WAY OF LOVE

WAY OF LOVE

*Recovering the Heart
of Christianity*

Norman Wirzba

HarperOne
An Imprint of HarperCollinsPublishers

HarperOne

HarperCollins books may be purchased for educational, business, or sales promotional use. For information please e-mail the Special Markets Department at SPsales@harpercollins.com.

HarperCollins website: http://www.harpercollins.com

FIRST EDITION

Library of Congress Cataloging-in-Publication Data is available upon request.

ISBN 978–0–06–238581–9

16 17 18 19 20   RRD(H)   10 9 8 7 6 5 4 3 2 1

For Gretchen—
companion in the way of love

CONTENTS

Part IV. Redemption

Part V. Hope

FOREWORD

A FEW YEARS AGO, I purchased a painting from a noted western artist. It depicts a lake in Wyoming's Wind River Mountains in a cool blue palette that signals the connection between water, earth, and sky. The picture invites viewers into contemplation of nature's reverie invoking both rest and renewal. When I first glimpsed the image in the art gallery, it literally drew me across the room. I knew that it was intended for me, as a beckoning icon of God's beauty. It now hangs in my living room as a reminder and celebration of creation.

But there is something not quite right about the picture. It is in the wrong frame. While the painting exudes a sort of calm azure holiness, the frame is a gaudy gold. The frame's edges are too wide and deflect attention away from the lake at the center, while its metallic sheen fights the subdued tones of the mountains. It appears as if the artist did not match the frame with the picture. Instead, he probably used the first frame from his storeroom that fit the painting's dimensions without thinking about the story the picture told. He took whatever was at hand and did not consider how it would—or would not—complement the image.

Every time I pass it on my living room wall, I think: "I need to change that frame."

That is, of course, how many people now view the Christian faith. The picture painted by Jesus is a beautiful one of healing, abundance, and justice. It invites people into God's grace and opens the eyes and heart to kindness, peace, and mercy in this life. Jesus was an artist of love and human flourishing; his canvas was the sacredness of the world. But something is wrong. It is as if the vision drawn by Jesus and intended for delight was put in the wrong frame. The structure around the picture and the picture itself are in conflict.

In these pages, Norman Wirzba reframes the painting. He reminds us that Christianity's focal point is a vision of God's love that creates, sustains, and redeems the world. Then, in each succeeding chapter, Professor Wirzba carefully strips away layers of gaudy paint on the four sides of the old frame—Creation, Fall, Salvation, and Heaven—and reworks and reuses the old pieces to construct a new frame that directs our attention back to the center of the canvas. In the process, both the painting and the frame spring to life as a way of love that draws readers into a greater sense of meaning and joy. And Christianity emerges from encrustations of doctrinal rigidity and institutional regulation as a path of the heart.

There will be some who think that both the painting and the frame are the problem. And others who think that Christianity needs a completely new frame and none of the old bits can be repurposed. These are conversations and arguments that the church needs to have. But, in the meanwhile, many Christians are longing for the old, old story to be told in a new, new way. And by recycling and refinishing the frame, Norman Wirzba demonstrates that the painting may not be the problem at all. It is possible to make all things new by reframing that which The Artist always intended: that love is the all in all.

For those of us who have known that we need to change the frame, *Way of Love* is a gift. It enables us to see—and experience—the painting afresh.

Diana Butler Bass
Alexandria, Virginia

PART I

Christianity as Love

Chapter 1

The Right Measure of Faith

Whoever does not love abides in death.
1 John 3:14

Does Christianity still matter? Aren't we better off without this archaic religion and its sectarian squabbles and divisive politics? Why even bother with God when it is clear that the idea of God is the basis for so much pain and hurt in the world?

This book is my attempt to answer these questions and to argue that Christianity very much still matters. Well, to be more precise, I will argue that the Christian faith *can* and *should* be taken seriously, provided that we rediscover Christianity's heart.

Christianity matters because it reveals the deep mysteries of God and the meaning of all life. It shows us what life is for and when it is at its best. And what is this ultimate revelation? The answer is surprisingly and profoundly simple: Christianity reveals the life of God and therefore also the meaning of life as *a way of love.* God, life, and love—these three are indispensable for a good and beautiful world. Without these three *together,* everything falls apart. That is the heart of Christianity, and that is the message we most need to recover.

This revelation about love is not obvious. One only has to point to the fact that we live in a world too much acquainted with love's opposites—hatred and violence, boredom and fatigue—to affirm love's centrality. Histories of war, genocide, and now ecocide suggest that love is rarely the ideal that inspires human hope and action. Doesn't the barbarity and indifference of just the last century, a century when we thought we'd finally behave at our enlightened best, only to devise and carry out unprecedented levels of killing one another, teach us that the reality of God and the life of love are delusions?

Moreover, a quick look at Christianity's history and some of its contemporary expressions demonstrates that Christians have not always lived out their faith as a "way of love." In fact, the church has at times shown itself as the enemy of love. This is at the heart of the crisis in the church today and explains why so many people have chosen to stay away or drop out. Christian leaders and their followers have often distorted love by turning it into a possession reserved primarily for themselves or those they deem worthy. By turning love into a stick used to exclude or punish others—women, children, minorities, foreigners, homosexuals, the homeless, criminals, or handicapped individuals have each had a turn at being the unwelcome "other"—Christians have often unleashed hatred into the world, not love. Christian-inspired hatred, however, is a theological catastrophe and a failure of massive proportions, since it runs counter to what the Bible explicitly teaches: "Those who say, 'I love God,' and hate their brothers or sisters, are liars; for those who do not love a brother or sister whom they have seen, cannot love God whom they have not seen" (1 John 4:20).

But recognizing the harsh realities of this world and pointing out how the church falls short of its ideals do not mean those ideals are wrong. No, my claim is that it is precisely these shocking experiences of the opposites of love that teach us that *life needs love* to lift existence out of the quagmire of neglect and brutality. Without love, life becomes a more or less tolerable descent into death. To give up on love is also to give up on the world and each other.

Additionally, *love needs God* to expose and explode the often anxious, often self-serving desires that are love's pretenders. After two thousand years it is easy to overlook just how revolutionary the gospel of Jesus Christ really is. The God revealed in Jesus of Nazareth introduces us to forms of love that turn customary ways of ordering life upside down and inside out, showing us that what people think about love is often far too narrow and far too small. Insofar as Jesus inspires genuine love in the world, life becomes an adventure in the ways of solidarity and celebration. Love is the crucial thing, because it is love that separates the ways of life from the ways of death.

Jesus stands for a perpetual revolution in the life of love, because he insists that all people, no matter who they are or what they have done, are invited to become children of God. Scripture is so shocking, because it reveals that the scope of Jesus's healing and reconciling ways extends to every square inch of the universe. There is no place or time where God's love does not seek to go. The love of God revealed in the life of the man from Nazareth explodes all the categories and classifications we use to devise who is "in" or "out," worthy or unworthy, because its reach is infinite, encompassing everything that is.

Love has always been a contested and fragile power, vulnerable to multiple forms of misunderstanding and abuse. Discerning the truth of love and the trustworthiness of Christianity's expressions must, therefore, go hand in hand. For too long, too many Christians have acted as if by simply reading scripture and adopting the name "Christian" they have been inoculated with the equivalent of a "love gene," thinking that they now understand love and that love will immediately flow from them. The history of the church and most people's experience of other Christians show this to be false. That is not how love works or how God works.

Though the Bible is all about revealing the logic of love, we must acknowledge that the study of sacred doctrine and scripture may not be enough to lead one to the truth of love, let alone help one become more loving. Scripture by itself cannot carry all this weight. The way of love requires a transformation of the human heart and a reorientation of one's life. To become proficient in the ways of love, we need a sympathetic and supporting community helping us all along the way.

Christianity is best understood as a training ground in the ways of love. That is what Jesus began and what he wants his church to continue to do. And since love is a subject that is not fully known by memorizing formulas or studying textbooks, we should not be surprised that the Bible often resorts to stories as the best vehicles for training disciples in the way of love, stories that invite us in and change us, so that we can live out this new way of love for ourselves. In the same way, throughout this book, I use not only stories from the Bible but stories from history as well as from our own time, stories that inspire, model, and train us in the ways of love.

For instance, what love requires from us and how our hearts need to be transformed are movingly illustrated in the life of Oscar Romero, the former archbishop of San Salvador. Romero came to this realization about the personally transforming nature of love in a profound but costly way. Having been raised a devout Catholic Christian and then having gone to Rome, where he studied theology and was ordained as a priest, he returned to El Salvador to do the work of the church. In his role as priest and then bishop, he assumed that the ways of God were in fairly close alignment with the priorities of the Roman magisterium and the Salvadoran government. For him, at this time, Jesus was not a revolutionary figure.

Romero saw in Jesus someone who could be used to defend his country's status quo.

The status quo of El Salvador depended on massive inequalities (nearly half of the country's land was owned by just over a dozen families) and the vicious suppression of pleas for justice. While church officials and government leaders lived in relative luxury and ease, the vast majority of the population's peasants struggled to find enough food to eat and a safe place to live. Though fellow priests had taken up the cause of these poor people, Romero sided with the wealthy, conservative leadership. When Romero was appointed archbishop of San Salvador, the country's leaders were pleased, knowing that he would not challenge or condemn the injustices that had become routine.

This all changed when Rutilio Grande, a progressive priest and Romero's personal friend, was assassinated for his advocacy on behalf of the poor. Romero asked for an investigation into the murder. His request was denied. Subsequent appeals to stop the government-sanctioned killing of priests and innocent people went unheeded. And so began a time of intense personal struggle for Romero. How could the goodness of the love Grande showed to others be met with such vicious and murderous hate? How could a church founded on the love of God stand by and let its priests be assaulted when they expressed their love for the people? Romero was beginning to see that the love of God compelled him to advocate for the poor. A heart transformed by love cannot sit idly by as people suffer oppression and abuse. Why? Because all such abuse is a rejection of and an assault upon the love of God at work in them. To fail to act is to betray the very love that Christians are called to embody.

It was by opening himself to the love of God expressed by the common people that Romero found the courage to change and align himself with love. He decided to live in solidarity with the poor and learn from them the ways of love and the ways of God. Poor people, rather than professors, would now be his teachers. Romero began to preach his Sunday sermons over the radio, sermons in which he condemned the abuses of power and the unconscionable greed of the country's leadership. These sermons were the most-listened-to radio program in the country. He even wrote a letter to President Jimmy Carter, asking him to stop sending military aid to right-wing paramilitary groups that were killing the peasants he loved.

Romero's criticism of the government and the church establishment made him a marked man. It was clear to him that people who wanted to preserve the status quo would now try to kill him and thereby silence his witness to the revolutionary implications of love. On March 24, 1980, while Romero was celebrating a Requiem Mass, a gunman assassinated him, taking his aim through the open doors of the church. In the sermon just preached, Romero had said that Christ's gospel teaches that

> one must not love oneself so much as to avoid getting involved in the risks of life that history demands of us. . . . Those who try to fend off the danger will lose their lives, while those who out of love for Christ give themselves to the service of others will live, live like the grain of wheat that dies, but only apparently. If it did not die, it would remain alone. The harvest comes about only because it dies, allowing itself to be sacrificed in the earth and destroyed. Only by undoing itself does it produce the harvest.[1]

As Romero had come to see, love does not allow people to flee or shield themselves from the pain or the troubles of this life. Genuine lovers move deeply into the life-and-death dramas of this world, like a plant that sinks roots deep into fertile soil, and there give themselves wholly to the flourishing of life. To withhold oneself from love is to withhold oneself from participating in a complete life.

The love of God presents each person with this paradox: abundance of life requires that people learn to give themselves away in service of others, for it is in this self-offering movement that life is fully affirmed, nurtured, and celebrated. Like a seed that is opened to receive the nurture of the soil, people must open themselves to the world so they can benefit and grow. Love is the outbound movement that trains people to heal injustice and kindly embrace the world. Nothing less than the sanctity of life and the grace of the world are at stake. This is the very foundation of the Christian faith.

An Essential Way

Our way into the fullness of life is the way of love. That is the central claim of this book. Love is the power that enables us to affirm, even embrace, the wide range of life's splendor and tragedy. It is the passion that enables us to protect, nurture, and celebrate every created thing. It is the lens that enables us to see each person and creature as a gift worthy to be cherished. Love is the eternal "yes" to life's possibilities and promise. It is the form of protest that says "no" to all the forces in our world that diminish and degrade life.

But how do we learn to love? How do we make sure we don't take wrong turns or pursue the wrong paths, as so many have done before us?

These questions speak to the perennial need for something like schools for the learning of love. Christianity is just such a school—or at least it was designed to be. It is an ongoing training session in which the many versions of love on offer are tried and tested.

In this book I return to Jesus's original vision of the church as a training camp for love. Seeing Christianity as a school or laboratory that trains people in the ways of love is the best way to understand the work and mission of the church. When the church is faithful to its calling, it offers the most extensive curriculum imaginable, because that curriculum touches every aspect of life and this world. It is an unusual school that lasts a lifetime and from which we never really graduate, because there is so much to see, so much to learn, so much to attempt. Christian faith is really one long apprenticeship in which we work to understand and then root out the many ways we devise for falsifying or simply denying love. It is the tradition of practice in which people refine the sympathies and the skills that enable an honest and complex embrace of the world. Love is the crucial thing. Without love we lose hope.

From a Christian point of view, love is the inspiration, the means, and the goal of life. It is the heart that pumps whatever genuine life Christian faith and practice make possible. Love is the crucial ingredient that makes a life worth savoring and the harmonizing presence that makes a song worth singing. It is the power that lifts even the most mundane acts into the realm of festivity, and it is the grace that forgives our waywardness and heals our brokenness.

When Christians forget this or think they can graduate early, their faith becomes a waste of time or, worse, dangerous. To fail to love is to lose God, the world, and each other. It is to bring needless suffering and pain into the world. It is to become an obstacle to creatures who seek to live into the fullness of their lives. To fail to love is to forfeit a life worth living.

I'm not the only one saying this. In one of the earliest accounts of the Christian faith, the apostle Paul, a man known for his great learning and piety (and formerly for his terrorizing of Christians) said: "If I speak in the tongues of mortals and of angels, but do not have love, I am a noisy gong or a clanging cymbal. And if I have prophetic powers, and understand all mysteries and all knowledge, and if I have all faith, so as to remove mountains, but do not have love, I am nothing" (1 Cor. 13:1–2).

Love or noise? Love or nothing? It is a stark choice, indicating that if Christianity is not fundamentally about enabling people to love, it should cease to exist. My aim in this book is not simply to suggest that Christianity has interesting things to say *about* love. Rather, it is to show that love is the *essential movement* that is the core and climax of life and faith. Christianity teaches that "God is love" (1 John 4:8). That means authentic faith is realized as people witness to and learn to participate in the love that is God's own life. Apart from a journey in this way of love, God remains unknown and life unfulfilled.

I expect that some will be surprised by what I say about Christianity. In part, this is because there have been multiple expressions of Christianity in which love has not been the center or the animating heart through which all its teaching flows. It is time for these forms of the "faith" to die. Though they may witness to considerable learning, piety, and power, these expressions of Christianity will finally be judged to be nothing.

This book is an account of how love gives shape and direction to Christian faith and how this faith helps us live better. With the word "better" I mean to encompass a lot: a life that is more *honest* with life's difficulty and potential; more *beautiful* and worthy of *respect* and *celebration,* because it honors and nurtures the potential blessing latent within everything; more *responsible,* because it acknowledges and seeks to correct the injustices in our world; more *meaningful,* because it affirms creatures as gifts worthy of our attention and cherishing; and more *hopeful,* because it is inspired by the divine love that first brought this world into being and that promises to bring an eventual end to its suffering and pain. Christianity deserves consideration, because it gives one of the most illuminating and compelling accounts of life and love ever produced.

Is the account I offer true and worthy of anyone's effort? To find out, you'll simply have to join in, bring your concerns and your questions, and see if Christianity resonates with you, perhaps even challenges you to think about life in ways you never considered. In contexts of cynicism, irony, and boredom, love looks foolish and ridiculous. What I hope to show is the reverse: a world without love makes our living a silly game in which the claim to be "successful" or a "winner" is finally meaningless. Love is the thing that makes life worth living. It is the power that brings light and warmth to a world that would otherwise be dark and cold. A faithful life, as we shall see, is simply and profoundly a life in which the love of God is made incarnate and active.

Not enough people see that this life and this world are beautiful and precious gifts of God that, however damaged they may be, are worthy of our cherishing and celebrating. Not enough Christians appreciate that love is the power that inspires their faith and makes their living a participation in the ways of God. *Way of Love* is not a comprehensive statement of all that Christianity is. Instead, it is an invitation to consider and experience the heart of Christianity, a heart that beats so that every person and every living thing can move into the fullness, beauty, and goodness of life.

CHAPTER 2

Love Lessons

Teach me your way, O LORD, that I may walk in your truth.
PSALM 86:11

MANY PEOPLE HAVE NO problem affirming the idea that love is at the center of what gives life meaning and satisfaction. But that does not mean they then take the next logical step and dedicate time to learning how to love. Why is that? Do we think that love is so natural and obvious that we do not need to be trained in it? Yet, as anyone who has experienced intimate relationships has learned, love is difficult. It takes work. We can be mistaken about what love is and what it entails, which is why we need other people and traditions of insight to teach us what love looks like and requires. Because it is so easy to be misguided about love, we each need ongoing education in the ways of love. Christianity is a training ground for precisely this sort of education. If love is the heart of

Christianity, then training in love must be at the center of what Christian faith is about.

Not long after I got married, a close friend called to ask, "Have you figured out yet how easy it is to hurt your wife?"

It was a real downer of a question. Here I was, still enjoying the afterglow of honeymoon bliss, when he set out to remind me that I would inevitably betray my love. I flatly denied that I would do such a thing. But I was fooling myself. In fact, I was lying.

His question haunted me. Eventually, I forced myself to look more carefully at the way I treated Gretchen. Looking back, I shake my head at all the ways I expressed my pettiness and arrogance. "Shouldn't the closets be organized this way?" There were little public humiliations when I cut her down or asserted myself as the boss. "She's a really good cook, but you should taste the way my mom makes it." Sometimes I was so wrapped up in my own concerns and worries that I was completely oblivious to what was going on in her life. "Come next fall, I'll have a job, we'll be living in a new place, and our lives will finally get started." As if Gretchen didn't have a life and goals of her own!

I wasn't trying to be malicious. Like many others I knew, I was caught up in the busy whirl of life, simply trying to make my way with my own agendas and my self-chosen identity intact. I had hopes for how I thought life should be: I would become a successful professor teaching at a good college or university. I had a vision and a plan for ongoing happiness that certainly included my wife: we would raise a family and be respected members in our community. Looking back, however, I now realize that I was not sufficiently attentive to her needs and potential, her hopes and dreams. I was the center of my world. Early on I realized that I had a lot to learn about how to love my wife.

Twenty-five years later, Gretchen and I are still married, even happily so. We are the proud and busy parents of four fabulous children. Experience, grace, and a patient commitment on Gretchen's part have provided me with much training in the ways of love. Reflecting on the course of our life together, I am frequently humbled by the forbearance and kindnesses that exist between us. I am regularly amazed by the joy that comes from our shared life. We have our struggles, but we also have a lot of fun. I now know myself to be blessed by a marriage, a family, and work that are better than I could have imagined, certainly better than I deserve. My life would be immeasurably impoverished without the love we learned to express and share. But that came from doing the work of learning how to love, work that has been steadily informed by what Christianity teaches us.

I haven't stopped repeating my friend's question to myself. I think it is an essential question. "Why is it hard to love others, but so easy to hurt them?" I need this question, because it is at the heart of why learning to love can be such a challenge and why we are in need of training in the way of love. We all need some spiritual equivalent of a map that helps us see when we are heading in the right direction, moving toward a destination that is beautiful, good, and life-giving, and warns us of the paths that lead to the harming or neglect of others.

To learn to love—this is the supreme, all-encompassing human task. It is, I think, the ultimate treasure worth searching and striving for, because it is the inspiration and the energy that makes every other objective worthwhile. It makes perfect sense that love is the great subject of the world's art, because when love is present and active, even in the most mundane situations, we feel more satisfied and alive. One could say that love is the bloom to life's flower. It is the power that makes life in this world valuable and meaningful. Without it we will likely become negligent, irresponsible, or destructive. That is what I have needed to learn over and over again.

One of the more painful lessons of my life has been to appreciate how the need to protect and preserve my sense of self has made it difficult for me to love and cherish the world around me. As much as I try to be gentle with and kind to others and as much as I try to be grateful for and nurturing of the gifts that make up my world, a basic need to self-promote or self-protect causes me to break faith with those around me. I don't usually set out to be mean about this. But for whatever reason, whether out of fear or resentment or out of arrogance or some latent insecurity, I want to set myself apart as beyond fault, even beyond question. The roots of this desire for self-preservation go deep. It is a desire that manifested itself in my life at an early age.

I remember one occasion when I was about eleven years old and enjoying a leisurely afternoon on our Alberta farm. I had been playing with my dog, Kalo, an energetic golden lab, when I spotted a sparrow sitting on an electrical line overhead. I had the perfect stone in my hand—farm boys are rarely without some weapon in their possession!—and figured I could easily hit the bird on the first try. I took aim and fired. Of course, I missed. But what I didn't miss was the rear window of my grandfather's car. The glass shattered into a gazillion pieces. I was horrified and scared. What was I going to tell my dad when he came home? I decided to take a well-practiced path: play ignorant, and if that doesn't work, go stupid.

When my dad asked about the window, I said it must have been a bird that did a nosedive directly into it. Upon hearing my explanation of how such a thing is likely, even inevitable as the only reasonable explanation, my dad simply said, "Impossible. You broke the window. You're paying to get it fixed." I began to make my case, suggesting that some birds really are mad and crazed creatures. They think nothing of killing themselves just so they can make our lives more difficult!

Then, an amazing thing happened. My grandfather, having just seen his broken car window and heard my lame explanation, walked up behind me and said, "I believe him. I can see that a bird might do that."

I felt momentarily relieved, but also profoundly stupid. Everyone knew I was lying. But my grandfather took note of my panic and felt pity for me. He made an allowance for my insecurity and fear and my need to present myself as beyond fault. He demonstrated his unfailing love for me by forgiving me and not holding my foolishness against me. He modeled what love looks like and what it will do in service of the well-being of another. I have never forgotten his love for me in that moment. I also have never forgotten my shame. It took several days before I mustered the courage to tell my dad and grandfather what they already knew. I promised to pay to have the window fixed.

In retrospect, this little episode shows how pathetic and irresponsible I could be in the promotion of my own life. I was engaged in the serious business of securing my position in the world. Since then I have continued in the pursuit of that same business. I now wonder what else I have shattered or damaged along the way. To answer this question, I have the instruction and the modeling of my father and grandfather to help me on my way.

Getting Started

LEARNING HOW TO LOVE is a long and complicated process. As I said in the previous chapter, I have written this book because I believe that Christianity at its best gives an honest, rigorous, and compelling account of *life as a way of love*. It gives us the metaphysical map we need by which to evaluate the wide sweep of potential human destinations in life. It helps us determine which destinations are worthy of our effort and which paths meet our needs for nurture and companionship and genuinely fulfill our desires for peace and joy. As a map of the human heart, Christianity shows us why some strategies or paths don't get us to where we think we are going and why some destinations are not really worth the effort, because they end up being places that leave us anxious or alone.

Though I have found that providing a field guide to the terrain of love is the primary point of Christian faith, Christianity was never presented to me in this way. I have learned many useful things over the years, but I was never given such a field map or training manual in the church that raised me or the divinity school that taught me. And so I have, with the help of others, been developing it as I go, trying to determine appropriate responses to the questions I think most important. After many years of study and practice, I am becoming more and more convinced that Christianity is designed to teach us vital things about how to live by showing us the potential and the difficulty of love. That is what I want this book to show.

I am not saying this is a new discovery. Many saints have written about the primacy of love, but their insight does not have sufficient traction today. It is too common for people to spend time in churches and not realize that the whole Christian enterprise is about training in and expressing love. That needs to be fixed.

I am aware that a recommendation for Christianity can be a tough sell. I meet the friends of my children and see that many of their contemporaries find the prospect of a Christian life either repulsive or simply uninteresting. My goal is to engage readers in a conversation on whether Christian faith can lead people into a deep and honest affirmation of life. I want to explore with others, including people of other faith traditions or no faith tradition at all, how Christianity can be a way of life that brings healing, goodness, and joy to our world.

A growing number of people find appeals to faith to be a nonstarter. For them the only debate about religion is whether to have the debate at all. Why bother with a religion that is often arrogant, contentious, or silly in its pronouncements? I sympathize with these sentiments. I too am skeptical about human abilities to know and understand even the most basic things in life, such as why we exist and why our world is saturated with so much violence and pain. I have learned to distrust religious leaders who are often more interested in elevating their own position or protecting whatever power they or their immediate tribe happen to have.

And I am not alone. More and more people within religious communities are becoming disaffected, finding their leaders unable to communicate a faithful way of life that is honest and inspiring, a way of life that is worth deepening and cherishing, and so they stop going to church. Though church buildings abound, many of them have ceased to be places where love is expressed and taught.

I believe the problem is not the faith itself, but that our structures have ceased to be inspired and moved by Christianity's heart. Christianity is supposed to be a way of life pointing us to a life of love, a life that is abundant and vibrant, but churches are struggling to provide compelling maps for guiding our steps. I hope this book will become such a map or at least a reminder of what the heart of Christianity is supposed to be. If we have good maps of the heart, we might be more able to determine how we got to where we are and how we can make sure we are undergoing the training we need. Then we will be able to move to some better place where life is cherished and celebrated.

When I was first learning to play guitar, I'd show up at my teacher's studio and play the selections that had been assigned for the week. After a few moments of awkward silence, my teacher often pronounced, "So you've just played some notes. How about you play some music?" At first I had no idea what he was talking about. I had played the notes mostly right and in a tempo that seemed appropriate, but a crucial element was missing, namely, the emotion and heart that make music worth listening to. I was playing notes without knowing—much less communicating!—what the music meant to me or what it could mean to others. Whether out of fear or plain technical incompetence, I was unwilling to let go and give myself to the song. I didn't trust the power and goodness of the music to flow through me. Apparently, it is possible to play the guitar and not really be playing music at all.

I think it is possible to show up in a human life and not really live it at all. I mean, you can have a good life "on paper," but then discover that what looks good on the page has hardly been lived from the heart and with a sense of the significance of what is going on. Like good music, a good life is one that is attuned to the joy and suffering, the beauty and the brutality of what we experience together. To play music in a way that really moves people, you have to give yourself completely to the song's depth and pathos, believing that in some way what you and the music are communicating is true.

In a similar way, to live a compelling life requires that you give yourself wholly to life's depth. You have to let life's goodness and sanctity take hold and move you from inside. But to do that you have to believe that life's sadness and pain and its surprise and mystery are worth giving yourself to. In other words, to give yourself unreservedly to others and to this world, you have to believe that they really matter and that they embody profound, perhaps even sacred, significance. Without trust in the fundamental worth and loveliness of life, it is hard to see why we should care about or devote ourselves to anything. That is what Christianity provides. It gives us entrance to a life in which the sanctity of things is front and center, a life that is truly worth committing to and cherishing.

Christianity at its deepest level gives us a vision of the world as the fully sensual manifestation of God's love and then provides us with the practices by which we can respond to this gift. It is an invitation to experience a life in which gratitude and contentment, peace and joy take their place alongside the difficulty and pain that will invariably come our way. Insofar as people are inspired and formed by the love that Christianity teaches, they become people who can live in the world with an uncommon appreciation for life's goodness and beauty. Christian faith that is working properly produces people who nurture and cherish life. It produces people who are fully alive rather than comfortably numb.

I first learned this from my grandfather Wilhelm Roepke, the same grandpa who forgave me for breaking his window. He was a German peasant farmer raised in the "bloodlands" of Eastern Europe during the world wars. The only life he ever wanted was one in which he took care of his land, his animals, his family, and his community. I came to see his work as one long labor of gratitude and devotion. But his was no simple life. He personally experienced as a soldier and then as a prisoner of war the unspeakable brutalities of war, destruction, and dislocation. Hearing the stories of the suffering, violence, and trauma he and his contemporaries faced, I came to wonder how he ever survived. He was separated from his home and family for months, not knowing whether his family and friends were alive, dead, or being subjected to pillage, torture, or rape. When he was finally reunited with his wife, two daughters, and a son, he had to live with loved ones who he discovered had been brutalized in ways that defy imagining.

When the war was over, my grandfather learned that he could never return to his farm; it had been confiscated by government officials. So he moved to western Canada in the early 1950s and vowed to make a new start. He bought land and worked to make it fertile and beautiful. He took care of his animals and fields. I remember once taking him to visit the Rocky Mountains that formed his western horizon. After a day of walking mountain trails and taking in stunning vistas, I asked him if this was not one of the most beautiful places on earth. He said, "It surely is. When will we be going home? I miss my home place." In him there was an uncommon congruence between what he wanted and what he had.

My grandfather was among the gentlest and kindest people I have ever known. He was fully present and alive to the gifts in his world. Despite all the pain and suffering he experienced, the joy and grandeur of life flowed through him. When I greeted him in the mornings, "How are you doing today, Opa?" he almost without fail said, "*Immer gut. Manchmal besser!* (Always good. Sometimes better!)" I loved being with him, because when he worked he often sang or laughed or simply marveled at what he saw. His bodily movements communicated contentment and humility. He didn't have to speak to express his gratitude and praise to God.

Having since learned more about the brutal world in which he grew up and then read some of the literature on posttraumatic stress, I now wonder how he did not become bitter, cynical, dis-affected—or simply shut down. Why was there no trace of apathy or resentment in him? How could he affirm life when he had lived through years in which a full-scale assault on it had been at-tempted?

The best answer I can give is that throughout it all he main-tained a steadfast trust in the goodness of God, a goodness that was apparent in the world around him if he opened and made himself responsible before it. He truly believed that, despite all the horror we can unleash upon the world, the love of God calls us to respond in acts of devotion and kindness toward each other. The astounding thing to me is that for him hatred of life or others was not an option. Neither was dishonesty or evasion. For him religious faith was not an escape from life's troubles. It was a way of participating in the redemption of the world. However it happened, my grandfather had been provided with a wonderful map that saw him through his life and directed him to live in particular sorts of ways. We all could use such a map.

My grandfather was training me in the ways of love, even if I did not know it at the time. Working with him was like undergo-ing an apprenticeship in love. His expression of faith, gratitude, and contentment taught me much about what it meant to live fully. He gave me a map I could follow, for which I am very grateful. I was his grandson, but also his student in more ways than I can fully articulate.

Learning in Community

WE CAN'T LEARN TO love on our own, because love is about nurturing and celebrating relationships. I often wonder if much of our confusion about love stems from the individualizing and atomizing forces in our culture. In multiple places—in schools, at work, even at home—people are taught that life is a competition in which others are frequently portrayed as obstacles to personal advancement. Or people are so busy that they don't really have the time to devote to the nurture and development of each other. And so many of us, despite being surrounded by people, often feel alone or as if we have to make it pretty much by ourselves. At the end of a long day, who has the energy and personal support to commit to training in the ways of love?

But life alone is a life without love. It isn't simply that people sometimes feel that they are not deeply and practically loved by others. It is that they lack the communal contexts in which love can be taught, modeled, and exercised. To learn to love, you have to practice with other people who are committed to inspire you when you are tired, celebrate you when you succeed, and comfort you when you fail. You need to see what other people are doing when they work at love and pay particular attention when the work gets hard, so that you can better prepare for your own attempts at love. You need to talk with others about what love means and requires, hear about past mistakes and successes, and learn from the memories and traditions that help communities thrive. All of which means that to learn the ways of love you have also to learn the ways of communal life.

Church is the name Christians give to the communal bodies that practice and promote the exercise of love. Church is the place where people come together to be inspired and taught by the love of God to act lovingly with each other and the whole world. Obviously, churches can fail terribly in this effort. But when they are functioning as they should, people discover that they are always loved, that they are responsible for each other, and that they are called to model to each other and to everyone the divine power that transforms fearful, bored, or lonely souls into people who nurture, protect, and celebrate the gifts of God. Christian community is the merciful and indispensable classroom in which people face their confusion about love, repent of their unloving ways, and switch from strategies of self-protection and self-enhancement to projects that seek the well-being of others.

It is easy for churches to fail in this work, because the love God calls people to practice and promote is sacrificial at its core. The love Jesus models is disturbing and difficult, because it represents an inversion of how we might ordinarily like to live. Scripture puts it this way: "We know love by this, that he [Jesus] laid down his life for us—and we ought to lay down our lives for one another" (1 John 3:16). Or as Jesus says it in John's gospel: "No one has greater love than this, to lay down one's life for one's friends" (15:13).

Love is not about gaining or securing the world for ourselves. It is about going to others and offering ourselves to them. It is about giving ourselves to others, so that our life together (and thus also we ourselves) can grow and flourish. Christianity hinges on the love that enables us to release our grip on ourselves as the central, most important thing in the world. But in order to risk loosening our grip, it is important to know that others will catch us when we fall or fail, support us, and help us get back on our feet again. That is what a thriving Christian community does. It trains people in the art of sacrifice.

Jesus shows through his own body and with his life that *the way of love is the way of sacrifice.* I can understand why this might not seem like good news. Loving others within the context of community life requires that we give of ourselves. This is a difficult thing to hear and appreciate, particularly in cultures and contexts that are governed by fear, shame, and abuse. Moreover, the vocabulary of sacrifice has been used far too often by people looking to legitimate their own ambition or oppress one group after another, such as when women are asked to "sacrifice" everything for their husbands and boyfriends or when young men and women are sometimes asked to "give their all" for a country at war. Like love, the language of sacrifice is susceptible to abuse. It can be the means for a denial of life rather than its flowering.

But the sacrifice inspired by Jesus does not ever mean the denial or degradation of life. It can't, because genuine sacrifice is the way of love, which is the way of leading others into the fullness and abundance of their life. Sacrifice is a communal, mutually abiding movement that strengthens life's relationships and potential. It is not a heroic or self-glorifying gesture. Though it may at various times lead some to a martyr's death—especially when the power of love comes face-to-face with the power of intense hatred—to "lay down one's life" for another does not mean that one is seeking self-annihilation.

Sacrifice means that we have made others the first priority and that we have joined ourselves to others, so that together we can be more attentive and available to the needs of the world. In the denial of self that Christianity recommends, we should not see self-hatred, because each creature is the expression of God's love. The love of Jesus calls us to look beyond ourselves, because without others we have no life. Life is a communion or membership of creatures in which each creature thrives to the extent that it is nurtured by others. If the membership is healthy and whole (because each member is committed to its nurture), then all the individuals within it will have the best life possible. Sacrifice is the gesture that keeps us focused on nurture rather than self-preservation.

To see the wide scope of sacrifice, we can look to John's gospel, where Jesus says, "Very truly, I tell you, unless a grain of wheat falls into the earth and dies, it remains just a single grain; but if it dies, it bears much fruit. Those who love their life lose it, and those who hate their life in this world will keep it for eternal life" (12:24–25). Here we can see that the movement of life is always transitive, taking us to others, binding us to others in relationships of mutual need and help. The moment we seal ourselves off from others or attempt to live solely from our own resources—perhaps thinking we are the source and destination of our own life—we perish in worlds of loneliness, deprivation, and death. The seed must give itself to the soil for the plant to grow. It must send its many roots far and wide so that maximum interaction and mutual benefit with its life-giving environment can occur. Like a grain of wheat, we must give ourselves over to the transformation and nurture that others can provide for us and we can provide for them. Life's fertility and vitality depend on the principle of self-offering that Jesus revealed in his ministry on earth. Self-offering is the crucial gesture that makes mutuality and togetherness possible.

Christian love teaches that life is not a possession to be hoarded or privately secured, because the way of possession inevitably leads to loneliness, isolation, and death. Life is, rather, a gift that is meant to be offered to and shared with others. Life and dispossession go together. Without the forgetting of oneself, the full flowering of life cannot occur. Christian life rests on this paradox: you find your life by giving it away. It is not a complex idea, but it is incredibly hard to perform, because personal fear and anxiety cause us to resist this self-giving. This is why we need a loving communal context that will inspire, teach, and nurture us to do it.

.

What Sacrifice Looks Like

To see what sacrificial love looks like and why a communal context is so important for its realization, we should look to the life of

Brother Luc and the monastic community in Algeria that instructed and supported him.

Shortly after midnight on March 27, 1996, Brother Luc was abducted from his bed at gunpoint. He must have heard the gunmen coming. It had been a long time since Brother Luc slept soundly. At eighty-two years of age, he was exhausted from years of tending to the sick who came to his monastery dispensary every day. But sleep came only intermittently, because painful asthmatic attacks made it difficult for him to lie down and get comfortable. He had made a routine out of propping himself up on pillows, so he could read and doze.

It is also likely that Brother Luc was kept awake by the presentiment that he would die looking into the face of his executioner. The monastery at Tibhirine, Algeria, had been the target of violent confrontation from area rebels before. The monks had been put on notice that their lives were not secure and that government officials would not protect the monastery. Brother Luc chose to stay with his brothers and with the people of Tibhirine. He continued to offer medical assistance to villagers and to those suspected of aiding various militant groups. He may have even treated men who at one time or another meant to kill him.

Brother Luc, born in 1914 as Paul Dochier, was no stranger to violence and bloodshed. While serving as a young military doctor in North Africa in 1939, he saw firsthand the horror and futility of war. Upon returning to France, he resolved to devote his life to treating the victims of violence. He wanted to be a healing, loving presence in the world. His resolve took him first to a German camp where—as a volunteer!—he tended to prisoners of war. It then took him to the Cistercian order. After several years of formation at the Abbey of Aiguebelle, he departed for Algeria, remaining there for the rest of his life.

Brother Luc could have chosen a medical career in France and enjoyed a life of relative comfort and success. But he loved the Algerian people, offering himself daily to them through acts of skill and kindness, and they loved him. He had learned from Jesus that a person who loves gives himself to others. And so he devoted himself to the care of the Algerian people, often seeing upwards of seventy patients each day in his little dispensary. Villagers held him in the highest esteem, because he made time for them, even when he was exhausted. He was commonly known as the *toubib,* the "doctor."

Nor was Brother Luc a stranger to abduction. In 1959 he was kidnapped by the National Liberation Army as part of a plan to bargain for the release of the imam of the mosque at Médéa. After a week of forced night marches, a rebel soldier arrived who recognized him as the *toubib* who had treated him when he was seriously ill. He berated Brother Luc's captors, telling them that this was the doctor who cared for the Algerian people. Brother Luc was quickly released. But his captivity had taken a toll on his health. He returned to France, so that he could recover and receive treatment for his asthma.

After returning to Algeria in 1964, he found that the monastery was no longer disturbed by the army. Along with his fellow monks, Brother Luc resumed the quiet, daily work of being a nurturing and reconciling presence in his community. Like a sprouting grain of wheat, he had given himself to the land and the people of Algeria. His self-offering was bearing much fruit in healed bodies, calmed minds, and mended relationships.

By 1996 Algeria was embroiled in a civil war that had been going on for several years. New threats to Tibhirine's people and its monastery were on the scene. Though a cheerful and jovial man, Brother Luc was no fool. He knew this time he might be killed. Not long before his abduction he wrote to a friend:

> **We can only exist as men by willingly becoming the image of Love, as manifested in Christ, who, though innocent, chose to suffer the fate of the unjust.**[1]

On May 21, 1996, Brother Luc was executed along with six of his brothers. His body was never found, but the heads of the seven monks were recovered on May 31. On June 4 he was buried in the cemetery at the monastery of his beloved community at Tibhirine.

Though committed to a life of simplicity and service, the monks at Tibhirine struggled with their presence in this war-torn region. They did not think of themselves as extraordinarily brave or good or righteous. Brother Luc's prior and fellow martyr Christian de Chergé spoke clearly to people's temptation to think of them as heroes:

> My life is not worth more than any other—not less, not more. Nor am I an innocent child. I have lived long enough to know that I, too, am an accomplice of the evil that seems to prevail in the world around, even that which might lash out blindly at me. If the moment comes, I would hope to have the presence of mind, and the time, to ask for God's pardon and for that of my fellowman, and, at the same time, to pardon in all sincerity he who would attack me.[2]

Rather than being heroes, these monks saw themselves as implicated in the suffering and violence of this world. They needed pardon as much as anyone else. They also needed constant encouragement and help, if they were to live in a manner faithful to their vows to be obedient to Jesus Christ. To continue to live and love in these difficult circumstances, these men needed to be reminded daily of the love that Jesus called them to. And for that they needed both the daily instruction that came from reading scripture together and singing the Psalms and the mutual support of their brothers. Brother Luc could not have done the work he did, if he did not know that his brothers were there to support him.

These monks were not seeking martyrdom. They loved life. They loved the people they felt privileged to know and serve. Where others thrived on mutual suspicion and fear, especially the suspicion and fear that was prevalent between Christians and Muslims, these brothers sought to build bridges and mutual understanding. Given their love for their Muslim brothers and sisters, they felt pained by the knowledge that their possible execution might become an occasion to enflame yet more interreligious hatred. Brother Christian spoke directly to this concern:

> I would not welcome such a death. It is important for me to say
> this. I do not see how I could rejoice when this people whom
> I love will be accused, indiscriminately, of my death. . . .
> Obviously my death will justify the opinion of all those who
> dismissed me as naïve or idealistic. . . . But such people should
> know that my death will satisfy my most burning curiosity. At
> last I will be able—if God pleases—to see the children of Islam
> as He sees them, illuminated in the glory of Christ, sharing
> in the gift of God's Passion and of the Spirit, whose secret joy
> will always be to bring forth our common humanity amidst our
> differences.

Though some would use the threat and fear of death as the means to keep people apart, Brother Christian sought only to find ways to encourage life together. But for life together to be possible, and thus also the hope of communal joy, these monks understood that they must first and always give themselves to those in their presence. To live life fully, they must practice the way of love, which is the way of sacrifice. Abiding in Jesus by following in his self-offering way inspired them to abide with others. In this mutual abiding they caught a glimpse of all people as children of God and all people as sharing a common humanity.

The witness of each of the monks of Tibhirine depended on a community of instruction and support. They couldn't do it on their own. They relied on liturgical rhythms and disciplines like daily prayer and shared mealtimes to keep them on God's way rather than their own. Above all, they depended on the Spirit of God casting out the spirit of fear that was ever present in their community. As the Algerian civil war came closer to the monastery, each monk had to face the temptation to flee or seek security through isolation. In the course of their deliberation Brother Christian read to his brothers the following passage from Christian Chessel, a friend and fellow monk who had been assassinated in Algeria in 1994:

> To accept our lack of power and our poverty is an invitation and an urgent call to create with others relationships that are not based on power; when I recognize my weakness, I can accept that of others, and see a way for me to imitate Christ. This attitude transforms our mission. It invites us to renounce all pretension of superiority in our encounters with others, however weak they are. . . . This attitude of weakness can be misunderstood. Weakness in itself is not a virtue, but, rather, an expression of the essence of our nature, one which must be molded and shaped by faith, hope, and love. To be weak is to be neither passive nor resigned; rather, it supposes courage and pushes us to struggle for justice and truth while resisting the elusive seduction of force and power.[3]

To describe weakness as our essential nature is not to denigrate human life. It is instead to be honest about the fact of our need. It is to acknowledge that for our life we always need others to be a source of nurture, comfort, and inspiration to us. It is above all to see how little we can provide for ourselves. Appreciating our weakness, we can then move into a frame of mind that rejoices in the creating, sustaining love of God. Others are the only soil in which we could ever hope to grow and thrive. This is why it is so important for us to learn to give ourselves to them. God is the power of love at work on the ground and in others enabling each of us to live up to our full potential.

It takes courage to surrender and give oneself to the "soil." What if the offering is rejected or abused? As the story of the monks at Tibhirine shows, what if the people one is trying to nurture return love with hate? It seems sensible and so much easier, or at least safer, to try to control and protect our own life, even if that means we will embark on violent paths to secure it. But as John's gospel says, to try to save one's life, either by withholding or locking it away, is also to lose it forever. As Brother Luc understood and demonstrated, a life with no regrets is one that has been given wholly to others. He said, "There is no true love of God without an unreserved acceptance of death."

Brother Luc did not desire to die. His desire was to live for others and find in their shared life the joy that makes life meaningful. But in the acceptance of death he communicated that the preservation of his own life—at what cost to himself and to others?—was not the most important thing.

To lose oneself for another is not to be diminished. It is, rather, to find oneself inspired by that other and in the mutual nurture that love creates find a greater fullness of life than could ever have been achieved alone. People sense this when they first "fall in love." When another enters your heart, you become more alive because your feeling and vision, your desire and purpose have been expanded and animated by the richness of the additional life. The beloved is not a threat to your existence. Instead, the beloved enters into you, giving you reasons to live in ways you may never have thought possible.

Brother Luc and his fellow monks found their reason to live in the land and the people of Algeria. Algerians had entered their hearts, opened them up, and then inspired them to experience the joys and pains of life together. Being together, they learned to offer themselves as individuals to each other and to the people of their community. Living together in a nurturing, instructing commu-nity that was shaped by the memory and witness of Jesus Christ inspired them with the courage they needed to face their own death; they each had to resist the temptation to let fear, envy, boredom, or hatred rule their living. By being together, they learned that it takes mutual nurture to give up one's presumed hold upon power and that it takes a loving community to empower one to be weak.

It is tempting to dismiss this story of martyrdom as something reserved for very special people, the superstars of love. This is a mistake. Brother Luc would insist that he was as ordinary as anyone. The brave and saintly things he did—befriend people who were lonely, treat people who were sick, act kindly with strangers—were clearly ordinary and within reach for anyone. Those things appear saintly to us because they were performed in such a difficult time.

Moreover and importantly, they were not the result of a solo Herculean effort. Instead, they were made possible by a community that instructed him and supported him daily in his attempts to be kind and merciful and helpful with others. Eating together, praying together, reciting the liturgy together, talking together, working together—all these enfolded within and inspired by deep traditions of monastic teaching and insight—became the training ground that facilitated the learning and the exercise of love.

Though you and I may not be called to become nuns or monks, the lesson to learn is that without participation in communities that instruct and train us in God's love, we should not expect to excel in the ways of love. It is impossible to predict the kind of love that is possible when people are formed and supported by a God-inspired community.

CHAPTER 3

The Drama of Love

Whoever does not love does not know God, for God is love.
1 JOHN 4:8

THE ARGUMENT OF THIS book, as we have so far seen, is that the point of Christianity, its central reason for being, is to communicate the unfathomable love of God that creates, nurtures, and perfects the whole universe, and then to invite everyone to participate in this love. This is a simple thing to say. But having been around Christians for a long time and having studied professional theology for decades, I have seen how often this is forgotten. Other concerns—for power, position, influence, or comfort—frequently usurp love as faith's animating center and goal. When love is forgotten or denied, Christianity fails. It becomes an embarrassment to God and a dangerous presence in the world. We can all point to examples.

The task of this book is to give a fresh presentation of Christianity, one that shows how Christian faith, including its diverse teachings and practices, is animated by, flows through, and is ultimately directed to the flowering of love. As the scriptures say, "God is love," which has more implications than we might at first realize. One implication, surely, is that Christianity is fundamentally about immersing people in the flows of divine love. It is misunderstood if it is seen as simply presenting some interesting teachings and tips *about* love. Love is not just one of several, perhaps optional themes that make up the Christian drama; rather, love is its animating core.

To use a building metaphor, love is the energizing and orienting foundation upon which the whole of Christianity rests. It is not simply one of the rooms that you might visit for a while or the outside decoration that might draw you in. Instead, love is the design principle and presence that integrates and powers the whole structure, giving it the appearance and functionality that it has. Without love, the whole house becomes ugly and useless. It simply falls apart.

But what does it mean to say that the heart of Christianity is a way of love, and what are the implications that follow? One implication, as mentioned in the previous chapter, is that we must commit ourselves to a lifetime of being trained in love, even as we actively seek to express that love. But that is not all. Even the way Christianity is presented, to those both inside and outside the faith, has to reflect love. How we see the world needs to reflect that love. How we see our role and purpose in the world needs to reflect that love. This chapter presents in outline fashion how love gives shape and direction to Christianity, and how it enables us to understand our role in the world. In the chapters that follow, the outline will be developed in greater detail.

The way we imagine this world, the expectations we have for a "successful" life, the diagnoses we give to life's problems, the hopes we cherish—all of these are decisively recast and reoriented when understood through the lens of love. From a Christian point of view, love and life are inseparable, because divine love is the pulse and power at work within everything. Nothing is possible and nothing makes sense apart from God's love. It is God's love that first *creates* the world. It is God's love that daily *sustains* life and *heals* it when it is wounded. It is God's love that *knits creatures together* into a membership or communion of life when things come undone. And it is God's love that *redeems* and *resurrects* the bodies of creation that have been degraded and wasted by violence and death. Love is the inspiration, the author, and the energy that moves the great drama of life. Without it we and the whole world face a futile and hopeless future.

It is easy to miss the deep significance of this love. God's love is not an afterthought or simply an action that God performs from time to time. "God is love" means that love is the ever-present, ever-active source and sustenance of all reality. The fundamental task of Christians is to *align their living with the divine love that is always already operative in the world*. Without this alignment, one can scarcely claim to know God at all. This is why it makes sense to describe Christianity as an apprenticeship in the learning of and participation in God's love.

But that is not how Christianity is often presented. What most people think of when the faith is summarized is a series of beliefs or statements of doctrine, such as in the Apostles' Creed, the Westminster Confession of Faith, or even the Four Spiritual Laws. And the problem with that approach is that love often disappears. Love fades into the background in these statements, because Christianity is presumed to consist first and foremost of a set of teachings or doctrines. Christianity is not, in essence, a set of teachings, but a *way of life*. Christian faith is a *vision of flourishing* that bears witness to God's love everywhere at work in the world.

Teachings clearly matter, but only insofar as they enable people to move into this way of life. When Jesus declares that he is "the way, and the truth, and the life" (John 14:6), he is not merely saying you better believe in him or else. No, he is showing a way to live and opening a path to follow him in the practice of his ministries of feeding, healing, forgiveness, and reconciliation. Jesus does not simply offer humanity a few teachings or model a few techniques for better living. He offers life itself, life in all its goodness and beauty, life in all its fullness and abundance. He shows us that the point of life is not merely to exist. It is to love.

Christian faith is an existential commitment or personal promise to perceive and live life in the kinds of ways that Jesus inspires and makes possible. For Christians, Jesus is the light that enables us to perceive the world as the material expression of love. He opens a practical path for people to follow, so that everything they do, everything they expect and desire is now in alignment with God's love. And that cannot be fully captured in doctrinal statements.

The joining of life and love is presupposed by much of the Bible, but clearly not all of it. There are places in scripture where violence is sanctioned, perhaps even encouraged, and there are some practices, like slavery and the harsh treatment of women, that are not seen to be a problem. The Bible is a complex book, containing multiple voices, not all of which are in obvious agreement with each other. Though it contains the revelation of God, it also witnesses to humanity's developing, sometimes struggling, sometimes erring discernment of who God is and what God requires. However, the overall structure and deep logic of scripture progressively communicate the miraculous and astounding nature of God's love. This love is so far-reaching and all-encompassing—so inexhaustible— that we should expect its revelation to be complex and frequently overwhelming. It takes time to appreciate.

That people often have difficulty understanding scripture is sometimes a feature of faulty reasoning or inadequate training. But an even greater impediment is the narrowness and smallness of our own loves, which prevent us from apprehending the radically inclusive and merciful love of God. Part of the problem comes from what we ask of scripture. If I believe Christianity is fundamentally a collection of true statements, then I will look for the Bible's "truths" and try to make sense of all of them. But if I see Christianity as a revelation and invitation to a way of life, then I will read scripture for the wisdom and guidance for living that Jesus and the biblical writers provide.

It takes time and a lot of practice to appreciate the love of God, which is why our readings of scripture need the correcting insights of others and the inspiration of God's Spirit of love to empower us to live in ways that witness to and extend the action of Jesus. For Christians, Jesus is the decisive window into the love of God and the logic of scripture. In his self-offering life we see where scripture has been heading and what it is ultimately about. Using another metaphor, he is the lens that brings the whole of scripture into focus.

Knowing the God of Love

IN JOHN'S FIRST LETTER, we read something that is startling: "Whoever does not love abides in death" (3:14). John presupposes that the love of life and the knowledge of God go together. Without love we simply cannot know God, because *the love of each other is our only access to God.* "Beloved, let us love one another, because love is from God; everyone who loves is born of God and knows God. Whoever does not love does not know God, for God is love" (4:7–8). This point is so crucial it is repeated: "God is love, and those who abide in love abide in God, and God abides in them" (4:16).

To say that "God is love" is an arresting claim, because it means that God is not some Superbeing out in the sky waiting to exercise (ruthless) power over everything. God has from the beginning been Emmanuel, "God with us," energizing relationships that nurture and heal whatever they touch. In certain respects, it makes more sense to characterize God as a verb rather than a noun, because God is the incomprehensible "action" that nourishes whatever action we or anyone else can perform. If our action does not flow within God's action, it is unlikely that God will be known or experienced.

In Matthew's gospel this point is made in a striking way. The scene is the time of an ultimate reckoning, when God, here described as a king, distinguishes between those who have truly been faithful and those who have not (Matt. 25:31–46). The deciding factor is not what people merely said or believed, but what they did (it is always the behaviors of people that are the more honest indicator of what they believe anyway). What God wants to know is if they fed the hungry, gave drink to the thirsty, welcomed strangers, clothed the naked, cared for the sick, and visited those in prison, because it is their love of others that demonstrates a relationship with God.

The supposed "righteous" ones protest, because they believe that the life of faith is what happens between God and an individual. It is a private affair and nobody else's business. But God has none of this. Echoing what we have already seen in John's letter, God says to these people that they can't possibly be doing anything to or for him if they are not already doing it to and for the people who surround them every day. If you want to claim to love God, you simply have to love the people that God puts in your path. "Truly I tell you, just as you did it to one of the least of these who are members of my family, you did it to me. . . . Truly I tell you, just as you did not do it to one of the least of these, you did not do it to me" (Matt. 25:40, 45).

This passage shows how God identifies with ordinary people in the midst of their daily struggles and troubles. God says, "I was hungry . . . thirsty . . . a stranger . . . sick . . . and in prison," because God is not aloof from the world, looking on disinterestedly from some distant height. If God is love, and love is the power that animates and nurtures all creatures, then God is present to every person. It makes no sense to sidestep the world in order to gain "direct access" to God. It's not simply about having a private, personal relationship with God, but about having an interpersonal relationship. To meet God you have to go deeply into the world and join with God's enlivening action already operative there in every creature. Love is the power that enables people to do precisely that. The test of faith is always the test of love: "If we love one another, God lives in us, and his love is perfected in us" (1 John 4:12).

The Structure of Christian Love

THE LOVE OF GOD resists simple definition. Love is, quite literally, unfathomable. In Old English a "fæthm" referred to the length of a person's outstretched arms and so became the roughly 6-foot measure used to establish the depth of a body of water. If you are moving through water, it is crucial to know its depth. Otherwise you risk running aground and coming to a crashing halt. If love is unfathomable, that means it can't be measured by us. We simply can't get our arms around it or reduce it to a size we can grasp. That is a supremely good thing, because it means that love isn't shallow.

Love is of such profound and inexhaustible depth that, no matter the size and weight of our troubles and dreams, love can always support and carry us. It is the medium so indescribably vast that there is no possible place we could be—even the depths of hell, as one of Christianity's classical creeds puts it—that love would not already be there. Love is the life-giving power that comprehends us without being comprehended by us. In it we move and have our being. In its infinitely outstretched arms we are not confined or coerced. Instead, we find ourselves lifted up.

To understand this love, we have to tell the story or drama of life. Of course, no single book could tell the unique dramas that represent all the individual journeys taken. But what we can do is group dramas together according to the kinds of plots they reveal. In other words, kinds of dramas can be found to show a similar narrative logic: stories that communicate the conditions for life's flourishing tend to follow a logic that is clearly distinguishable from stories that communicate the circumstances in which life falls apart.

When Christians have summarized the core movements of their faith story, they have often resorted to a fourfold structure that begins with God's *creation* of the world. This is a good and beautiful world that is made for the flourishing of all life. But human sin, as reflected in the pride and disobedience of Adam and Eve, the prototypical human pair, brings about the disruption and distortion of this goodness. The whole creation is said to *fall,* meaning that the relationships that join creatures with their Creator are fractured and broken. But the desire of God is such that God wants to see these relationships repaired and restored, and so God works to bring about the *salvation* of creatures. There are many facets to this saving work, but the overriding aim is for all creatures to be in a healthy relationship with God, for in God the fullness and perfection of life are to be found. When this happens, life is consummated and achieves its completion in *heaven*.

There are many reasons to applaud this summary of the faith. It has the virtue of being compact, fitting in multiple currents of the flow of God's life and humanity's response to it, and it conveys the dramatic character and movement of the life of faith. But it also misses something important. With this structure, it is easy to forget that the core movements within Christianity are fundamentally movements within the world of love: God's love for creation, our distortion of this love, God's training us in the ways of love, and love's fulfillment in the flowering of all life. When love ceases to be the core, the four movements, no matter how sophisticated in their presentation, are liable to take us off course.

In this book I want to keep love clearly at the center of the presentation of the faith. The fourfold structure of faith is recast, so that it becomes clear how the love of God or its rejection or distortion is at work in each movement. The wide sweep of life is presented through dramas that cluster around the broad themes of life created, wounded, healed, and resurrected. In each of these dramas, distinct dimensions of love's character and love's difficulty come to light. By attending to the role of love in each of the four parts—how love is born, is denied, is made operative, and ultimately becomes all in all—we begin to appreciate in fresh ways the deep significance of this life and this world, and we learn to appreciate how Christianity is a compelling and coherent way of life.

The four parts of this book that follow develop the four movements of love in Christian faith:

Creation: A Christian understanding of life begins with God's creation of the world as an expression of love. Nothing in this world has to exist. That anything exists at all is because God's love is hospitable, making room and space for creatures to flourish and grow fully into the life that is uniquely theirs. God's love is the power that initiates life and keeps it on the move. Understood deeply, creatures on earth are God's love variously made visible, tactile, fragrant, audible, and delectable. Life is precious and meant to be cherished. Everything and everyone are eternally and daily loved by God and are thus also eminently loveable by us. *When love becomes flesh, life is created.*

Fall: Because love is the power that moves the world, it is also the power people most want for themselves. When love is distorted, it then easily turns into forms of control and abuse. The moment people try to possess love and turn it into a tool they can use for their own advantage is also the moment in which needless pain and suffering are introduced into the world. The moment people refuse or turn away from love is the moment life comes apart. The world is damaged and life is wounded when love is perverted or neglected. *When love is denied, life falls apart.*

Redemption: But God has always and only ever wanted life and love to flourish together. The Bible teaches that, from the beginning,

God has been at work to heal our diseased ways, mend our brokenness, nurture our need, reconcile our divisions, and redirect our waywardness. One of God's names is Emmanuel, "God with us," because God is forever desiring to lead all of creation into the fullness and joy of life together. In the person of Jesus of Nazareth, God dwells in the very flesh of embodiment, so that the whole world can be healed from inside. *When love goes to work, life is healed.*

Hope: The miracle of God's love is that life does not finally end in death. The love that first created life from nothing is also the love that re-creates life out of death. Though violence and pain and suffering are everywhere, these grim realities do not have the last word. Jesus's resurrection on Easter morning, his bodily ascension to heaven, and the promise of his return are all material signs that God intends *all* created bodies to share in the divine life characterized by love, joy, and peace. Heaven is not pie in some faraway sky. It is fullness of life with God and with each other. Heaven has an earthly life in which we are all invited to participate. *When love is "all in all," life is heaven.*

Put in summary narrative form: God's love creates a beautiful world, but our distortion and denial of this love lead to life's degradation. God does not give up on us or any creature, and so God works to redirect our waywardness, so that we can participate with God in the healing of all life. The goal of God's love is for it to be fully active in the life of each and every creature. When that happens life becomes heavenly.

Is this story true? Is this drama compelling? I don't believe these questions can be answered in the abstract, at the level of ideas. The truth of Christianity is borne out in its living. The power of Christian love becomes compelling as it takes on flesh in the lives of real people.

The chapters that follow develop some of the key moments in Christian faith expressing differing aspects of the movement and logic of love, examining them to see whether they help us understand and more honestly face the breadth and depth of our life together. Stories from people around the world help us see the difficulty of love and show what it means, and what it takes, to share in God's love for everything. The four movements of life created, life wounded, life healed, and life resurrected are expanded with the hope that at this book's end you and I will have a deeper understanding of how Christianity opens us to the beauty and the difficulty, the grace and the grit of love's way of life. This fourfold structure can serve as a powerful map, a field guide to the terrain of love, and so train us to live more faithfully in the world and with each other.

PART II

Creation

CHAPTER 4

When Love Becomes Flesh, Life Is Created

Everything has being through the love of God. . . . God is the creator and the protector and the lover.
JULIAN OF NORWICH[1]

WHY IS THERE SOMETHING rather than nothing? What is anything for?

From a Christian point of view, these questions are answered best in terms of the love of God. It is possible that nothing should ever have come into being. So the fact that things exist at all is because God loves and wants them to be. And because God is love, God is not content that things merely or barely exist. God wants everything to be beautiful and whole, and God wants every living thing to flourish and fully develop its potential. This world and this life are not a random fluke. They are the love of God become flesh, become active. Love is the inspiration, source, and goal of every-thing that is.

To appreciate this is to perceive and engage everything in a fundamentally new way. The Christian drama of faith begins with God's creation of the world, because it is here that we learn to ap-preciate that *love alone is the foundation of and medium in which all life participates.* When we begin to understand this, the rest of Christian teaching is cast in a profoundly new light.

Something very important about God's love is being commu-nicated here: God does not keep love as something to be hoarded or jealously enclosed within itself, but instead wants to share and extend to others all the goodness and joy that God's eternal life is. Love is not meant to be hidden, locked away, or enjoyed in secret. God's love constantly flows outward and offers itself to others, so that they can participate in the joy and delight that love brings. It is as though God, while enjoying a life more splendid than we can imagine, says, "The glory of my eternal life is so fantastic, it needs to be shared. But because nothing else exists, I first need to create beings so they can enjoy it too. I need to create the conditions in which the love that I am can be seen, touched, heard, smelled, and tasted." Think of creation as an immense, lavish feast in which God, the First and Essential Cook, has concocted such wonderful flavors that God wants to make creatures of every kind to taste them. And because it is a feast, the more the merrier. The only note of sadness would be to discover that there are some who missed the feast or rejected the delectable gifts made available.

The most important thing to say about the world and its life is that *God creates them.* To believe that worms and butterflies and dogs and people are *creatures* and that this earth and the whole universe are God's *creation* is to believe that everything and everyone has pro-found significance and, therefore, is worthy of our care and celebra-tion. Each and every thing, whether animate or inanimate, matters, because God desires them to be and loves them for who they are.

Things exist because God thinks they are wonderful. How could they not be, since they are God's love made material?

It is common for Christians to forget this. Sometimes they act as if only people matter or only certain kinds of people, and then perhaps only their ethereal, disembodied souls. The teaching of creation is one of Christianity's most radical and underutilized teachings, because it affirms that from the beginning everything is enfolded within God's love. It is not enough to say that God got it all going a long, long time ago. What needs stressing is the realization that creation is the temporal embodiment of God's eternal love.

This is a shocking thing to say, because it means that everything we encounter exists only because God's love is active within it, holding and sustaining it in its existence. No created thing or person is an accident or a waste. Instead, every creature is precious, because it is God's love variably made visible, tactile, fragrant, auditory, and nutritious. Moreover, nothing will be discarded or lost; God's eternal desire is for each and every creature to be reconciled by and gathered up in the love that Jesus embodied in his life. The most fundamental human task—because it frames the rest of what we do—is to learn to perceive the world in this unique way and then to develop the appropriate sympathies and responsibilities that will enable us to live harmoniously with others.

It is easy to miss the profound practical significance of this teaching, because people, Christians included, are tempted to think that creation is primarily about how the world began a long time ago. When creation is presented this way, people obsess about exactly how long ago God created things and by what means or method. This is a mistake. The Bible shows little interest in the scientific mechanisms that can be thought to have brought the universe into being. The important question is not, "How did the world originate?" but "Why does anything exist at all and for what purpose?" In other words, rather than being an investigation into the mechanics of origins, scripture presents creation as a material realm that has its inception, sustenance, and fulfillment in God. The point is not simply to look back to some originating point in time, much less to squabble about whether that was roughly 13.8 billion or 6,000 years ago, but rather to look around and look forward to see how the love of God is being realized or denied in whatever is happening.

Creation is a teaching about the *character* of the world and this life. As such it gives us something like a spiritual topography or a moral map that enables us to perceive the significance and value of whatever and whomever we encounter. It is a map that only makes sense in terms of God's love. Love tells us where things came from and where they are going. With this map we have an opportunity to appreciate how creatures best relate to each other and how together they are moving toward a future of mutual flourishing (or not). Maps orient us in the world, telling us where we are, and give us destinations that are worthy of attention and effort. They help us see when we are on paths that lead to no good end.

This is not to say that the teaching of creation gives us a predetermined world or that it provides a precise blueprint that lays out every step for our lives. The nature of God's love is to delight in improvisation as creatures respond to each other and to diverse contexts in creative, fresh ways. As we will see, to love is not to coerce, but rather to nurture and empower creatures with the freedom to pursue their own ends. What a teaching like creation does is give people a sense for God's presence in and hope for life. It lets us know what God thinks of this world, what God thinks it means, and also, as the ministry of God's son Jesus Christ demonstrates, what appropriate living within it looks like. It serves as an invitation to humanity to join with God in the work of furthering a beautiful and flourishing world.

The teaching of creation serves as the beginning of the drama of love not because it takes us to the first moment in time, but because it takes us to that most fundamental place from which the deep meaning and significance of things emerge. Is the world a vast realm of precious gifts or a massive store waiting to be shopped? Are the things of this world little more than commodities or natural resources to be used up? Are people reducible to pawns in the various plays for power that make up our political and economic worlds? As Part II will show, to receive and engage each other *as creatures* is to welcome, nurture, and celebrate the love of God made material in them (as, for instance, when we learn to be attentive to creaturely need, Chapter 5, and learn to act hospitably in the world, Chapter 6). But to be able to do that, people first have to learn to perceive the world and understand its meaning in an appropriate way.

Created from Nothing but Love

As CHRISTIANS TRIED TO make sense of God's creation work, they concluded that the world comes to us *ex nihilo,* "from nothing." Why insist on this point? Creation *ex nihilo* is a profoundly important but easily misunderstood teaching. To ancient philosophers, for instance, the idea was absurd: it is impossible for something to come from nothing. Their mistake, however, was to think that this idea was a scientific formulation. It isn't. To say that all creatures come "from nothing" is not to give a causal account of some "nothing" out of which things then come. It is, rather, to assert that there is nothing that compelled or constrained God in making anything. God did not have to create. God lacks nothing. God is not constrained by anything. The *only* reason things exist is because God loves them into being, which is to say that creation is *ex amore,* "from love." Creation is God's free act, the spontaneous eruption and the material manifestation of the eternal love that is the core of the divine life. Everything that exists is gratuitous and is a witness to God's incomprehensible and miraculous love.

The great mistake when thinking about God as the Creator of

the world is to imagine God as a Superbeing, the biggest, strongest, and most inventive Agent or Cause of the universe. Such a being is not God. It could not be, because if God is the Creator of the whole world, then God cannot be some object or being within it, no matter how large or magnificent or powerful we might imagine such a being to be. Stated in its most literal and shocking formulation, *God is no-thing,* because whatever "thing" there is only exists because God makes it. God is not one creature among other creatures. God is the Creator of them all. God is prior to and more fundamental than any particular thing, which also means that God and creatures exist on two fundamentally different planes of reality.

To say that God is no-thing does not mean that God does not exist. It is, rather, to affirm that God's existence or reality is of a kind radically unlike what we know and experience in our universe. This is a good thing, because if God's existence were like our own, God would thereby become a contingent, finite, dependent being, just as we are. If God was a creature, God would be unable to be present and relate to everything as its Creator. God is not a being on a continuum with other creatures. Instead, God is, as the medieval theologian Thomas Aquinas once suggested, the incomprehensible "power" or "action" that enables anything "to be." Whatever exists does so only because it participates in God's hospitable, enlivening power.

If God is not a creature, then it makes no sense to say that God "causes" the world to be, especially if we understand by causality the kind of phenomenon studied by mechanics. Causality presupposes two finite realities on a shared continuum or plane of reality that allows them to affect each other. For cause and effect to be operative they must, like two balls on a pool table, share the same world. The one must be capable of *infringing* upon the other in some way. The teaching of creation *ex nihilo* precludes this possibility. The reality of God and the reality of the world are radically discontinuous.

It is tempting to conclude that this abstract, philosophical point about the incomprehensible reality of God the Creator is a denial of all we have been saying about God's presence to, intimacy with, and delight in creatures. The opposite is the case. Because God is not confined to being one creature among many and thus only available to those creatures in close proximity, God can be present to every creature at the same time as the power undergirding and supporting all reality. Moreover, it is precisely because God is not an object or creature—no matter how magnificent—that God can be said to "exist" in a noncompetitive relationship with creatures. Because God does not in any way compete with creatures for their reality, creatures can be free to become who they are. This is a crucial point.

God is not made great by the diminishment of creatures (as would be supposed by a competitive relationship). Nor is God made less by any creature's flourishing. Instead, as creatures more fully achieve their potential—by accepting and nurturing the gifts God freely gives—God is glorified. As Irenaeus, one of Christianity's earliest theologians, once put it, the glory of God, what we can also describe as the full flowering of God's love, becomes most evident in human beings living abundantly into the life that God has given them.

The affirmation of the incomprehensibility of God is of immense spiritual and practical significance. If God does not "exist" in the same ways that creatures do, then God does not cause creatures to be, as we might cause a house or some artifact to be. Our ways of "creating" things invariably means that we exercise power over them. For us causality means a coercive and manipulating presence. But God's creating power does not operate at the level of domination or coercion. It moves on the level of love, which is to say that God creates out of the joy that delights things into being. God is the supremely gracious host and the lavish gift giver who withholds nothing for the good of the guest who has been welcomed.

God relates to the world not as a mechanic who manipulates matter to achieve an end. Rather, God relates to the world as a lover.

God does not make or force the beloved to become something or someone, for that would be to try to control the beloved. As the original and originating Lover, God is the nurturing, encouraging, sustaining presence that is forever working to uphold those who are loved as they attempt to realize their own potential. As such, God the creating Lover is always near but never nosy, always intimate but never intimidating. The love of God sets creatures free to fully become themselves. This point can hardly be emphasized enough.

If God's love is the only reason for the existence of everything, that means no one—no politician or teacher or parent or enemy or friend—can say that we exist for a reason other than to love and be loved. People might be told that their lives are worthless, because they don't contribute much to society or the economy's GDP, but that is a lie. Others might be told that their lives are a success only insofar as they achieve the goals others have set for them, but that too is a lie. The life of each person is only to be evaluated with regard to its participation in the ways of love, because it is only love that calls the world into being and allows us to make sense of it. You are good, because God desires you to be, and what God most wants is that you be empowered to realize the fullness of all your potential. It is hard to imagine a more liberating and inspiring belief than that.

To say that God creates *ex nihilo* is, therefore, to say that creation has always only ever been "from love." Every creature is an inexplicable gift that did not have to be. That anything is at all is only because God loves it to be. The world of creatures is one vast witness to a primordial, inexplicable, undeserved, noncoercive love. It is a love that circulates through everything and has the power to inspire and call to judgment our own attempts at love.

Creation *ex nihilo* is a crucial teaching, because it warns us not to confuse the reality of Creator and the reality of the creature. It is only as we appreciate God's transcendent, mysterious reality that the miraculous, liberating, and life-giving character of love has the opportunity to dawn on us. To be confused about God—as when we conceive God as a Superbeing who exists in a controlling, causal relationship with the world: the domineering Father, the unforgiving Judge, the micromanaging Engineer—is to be confused about love and to turn it into a coercive power that is exercised over others. The creating love of God teaches that *love never dominates what it loves*. If we don't understand this, our confusion results in our turning the world into an arena of competitive and manipulative striving. How much of the world is damaged and how many people are among the walking wounded, because we have failed to appreciate the noncoercive character of God's love?

Perceiving Creation

HOW PEOPLE PERCEIVE THE world is of supreme importance, because "what" we see determines "how" we are going to live in it. If the world is perceived to be a joke, an accident, or an arena of meaningless struggle, then we will have vastly different expectations and responsibilities than if the world is perceived as precious and destined for eternal life with God. To see the world as God's creation is fundamental to anyone's entrance into love's way of life.

Multiple reasons can be given for why people might not perceive this world as God's gift. Considering the long arc of evolutionary development and then witnessing the pain and suffering that runs through it, we are tempted to think that the best we can or should do is "survive." Assuming we are living in a world where there is not enough—we see scarcity at every turn—we are likely to develop a desire to grasp and hoard for ourselves as much as we can. Seeing once beautiful bodies fail or become disease-ridden, we naturally tend to think that the material world really is a vale of tears or perhaps a cruel joke. Like Socrates, we may learn to prefer death, so that our immortal souls will finally be released from the material bodies that cause us so much trouble and grief. Or we might prefer the contemporary equivalent promoted by futurists, like Raymond Kurzweil, who promise a similar flight from embodiment, this time not as an immortal soul, but as an information pattern that has been downloaded into a software program that can then be uploaded into limitless machines across the universe.

Christians have not been immune to the temptation to denigrate and flee this world. Throughout Christianity's long history and well into today, they have often been guilty of denying that the world is God's creation and that every creature is intensely and intimately loved by God. They have sought a supposed bliss in some ethereal heaven and thus presupposed that salvation means something like an escape from this world. Some even think the world is destined for destruction and oblivion. The maps guiding their lives do not take them more deeply and carefully into the world at all; the only direction those maps give is the suggestion that they get out.

This is a tragic mistake of the greatest proportions. It is a mistake that leads to a fundamental contradiction: the claim to be faithful to God while rejecting the material manifestations of God's love. Can a person profess to love God and at the same time consign God's beloved creation to oblivion?

To deny or degrade the material world is to deny and degrade the divine love that sustains and circulates everywhere throughout it. It is to misunderstand the God who is always near to creatures as a gardener is near to his or her garden. It is to forget that God became supremely near in the human body of the person of Jesus, who dwelled physically among us and in his dwelling showed us how to be creatures who welcome fellow creatures into the life of God. It is to deny the ongoing presence of God's Holy Spirit as the spirit of life that inspires people in the ways of healing and communion. And it is, fundamentally, to reject the orientation of God's own map, an orientation in which God's eternal love moves down permanently to earth, because it is with mortals that God forever wants to dwell

(Rev. 21:3–4). Any and all directions for life that prompt people to look away, disdain, or flee from this world reflect a distortion of the love that is always drawing God nearer to us.

Now we come to a crucial point. If we want to understand the love that brought the whole universe into being and that daily sustains it in its life, we must turn to Jesus, because Jesus is God's love made flesh and made practical. Jesus is the interpretive key that enables us to unlock the meaning and the significance of everything that is in its relationship to God. This is why the early Christian community declared Jesus to be the Creator of the world: all things in heaven and on earth exist through, in, and for Jesus (Col. 1:15–20). Jesus, we can say, is the one who helps us draw and read the maps of the world in a faithful and loving way.

Christians have long referred to Jesus as the "light of the world," because it is through him that we most fully move into the position where we can perceive and receive the world as God's creation and gift. In the opening to John's gospel, for instance, we read:

> In the beginning was the Word, and the Word was with God, and the Word was God. He was in the beginning with God. All things came into being through him, and without him not one thing came into being. What has come into being in him was life, and the life was the light of all people. The light shines in the darkness, and the darkness did not overcome it. (1:1–5)

Jesus is the light that removes the darkness in our world. He is the lens that brings creatures into focus, enabling us to see others as cherished by God. Jesus is uniquely positioned to do this, because he is not merely a human being. He is the eternal, divine Word, who has been with God from the beginning. As such he is also the one "through whom" all creatures come into being. Christ enables us to see life as created, because he is one with God the Father in being the Creator of all.

This is a remarkable thing to say. Why should anyone believe that a particular human being who lived in Palestine nearly two thousand years ago is also the Creator of all time and space? The answer is because the life of Jesus the Son is believed to coincide with the life of God the Father. Responding to the disciple Philip, Jesus says, "Whoever has seen me has seen the Father" (John 14:9). As Christians understand it, to look at Jesus's earthly life is also to see God's eternal, creative, loving life. Jesus enables us to see everything as God's creation, because in his ministries of feeding, healing, and reconciling we are given a practical, embodied demonstration of what life is about and what it is for. That is what Christians mean when they say that Jesus is God incarnate. The love he showed in Palestine for a limited time is the exact reflection of the eternal, hospitable love of God that first brought the world into being and that daily sustains it even now.

As both a human creature (begotten but not made, as the creeds sometimes say) and as our Creator (the eternal Word), Jesus is the utterly unique one who shows us what it means to perceive and receive life as created. Jesus can be trusted as the guide to a proper perception of created life, because he understands it from within as the love that moves in every breath, no matter how faltering, and within every material body, no matter how wounded. Jesus is the embodied love that bridges the chasm between the Creator and the created, between heaven and earth. In him the fullness of human and divine life come together, giving us a profound look into the meaning of both.

Attending to his life, we discover that the world can only be received as a gracious gift when people first empty themselves of their ambition, conceit, and their desire to turn a gift into a possession. In a startling passage, Christians affirmed that even though Jesus was "in the form of God," he did not view his divinity as something to exploit for his own purposes. Rather, Jesus "emptied himself, taking the form of a slave" (Phil. 2:6–7). Though Jesus had at his disposal the power of life and death—meaning he could be as coercive and domineering as he wanted—he chose to live in the world as a humble servant attending to the needs of all he met. He does not hoard divine love for himself, but constantly shares it with others. In him we see that the love that creates the world is also the love that welcomes and nurtures others, so that their life can be made complete. In other words, Jesus is the full and practical expression of what divine hospitality looks like. Insofar as people have "the mind of Christ" (Phil. 2:5), they will share God's hospitable, nurturing ways with creatures.

To summarize, when people believe that the world is God's creation, they are not simply saying something about its origin and thus referencing a belief that is only of tangential interest. No, the doctrine of creation is one of the most far-reaching and practical teachings, because it encourages people to perceive everything in a fundamentally new way—as God's love made material—and thus also to live in it such that all creatures are welcomed, nurtured, and celebrated.

CHAPTER 5

Creation Garden Style

And the Lord *God planted a garden. . . .*
Genesis 2:8

IF YOU WANT TO know the meaning of life—why it is, what it is for, and why it matters—and if you want to see what God's creating love actually looks like, one of the best places to go is to a garden. The biblical Garden of Eden is one such place (we will turn to it shortly). Another is The Lord's Acre, a three-quarter-acre garden nestled in the mountains of western North Carolina. As with its biblical counterpart, stories happen there that illuminate our most basic questions about ourselves, our world, and the purpose of things. Gardens are places where we face the fundamental character of our lives: our need for nurture, beauty, companionship, and good work. Gardens give us unique access to the lay of the land that is our life and world. Doing godly gardening work, we become apprentices in the ways of love and develop the habits of attention that enable us to know the world in a more faithful manner.

Started in 2009 by a group of concerned community members as an effort to provide fresh, poison-free food for poor people, The Lord's Acre has become something like the community's loom, weaving together people, plants, soil, and energy into a some-times messy, sometimes beautiful tapestry. When this community's people come together to work, eat, or simply enjoy the beauty of the place, the potential and promise of the community come into view. As Susan Sides, a writer for *Mother Earth News* in the 1970s and 1980s and the current garden manager, puts it, the garden has become a place where the diverse physiological, social, and spiritual hungers of people can be identified and addressed. When done right, gardens are places where God's love becomes beautiful, nutritious, and tasty.

But hunger is a complex thing. All creatures, simply by being alive, experience it. If nothing was hungry for food or intimacy or meaning or peace or adventure, would anything move? Life and hunger are inseparable, each one propelling the other. Hunger is what moves us forward. Hunger's omnipresence, however, does not guarantee that we understand it. We can be in the midst of profound personal or social hunger and not know its nature, why we feel it, or what will satisfy it. To see what I mean, consider the story that Susan tells. As in the biblical story, it is about misappropriated fruit.

One year garden members decided it was time to grow a few sweet melons. Roughly a dozen beautiful melons were getting ripe, when the garden interns began to notice that a few went missing. They were puzzled. Were animals eating them in the night? Then one morning they discovered all the remaining melons were gone. They also discovered a large pink cloth bag hanging on the shed. In it they found a bottle of beer and one of the melons. They removed the melon, but left the beer. The next morning the bag was gone.

Days later at a grocery store one of the garden interns spotted the same bag on a woman's shoulder. This woman—we'll call her Emma—was known to the gardeners as a neighbor who struggled with illness, poverty, and isolation. They assumed she was hungry and needed the food.

Several weeks later, having forgotten about the melons, Susan came to the garden and saw Emma helping herself to a pile of fresh produce. Wanting to understand her better, Susan struck up a conversation. After a short while Emma admitted to stealing all the melons and other produce besides. She described herself as ill and hungry and said that her landlord was often angry. In addition to looking out for herself, she thought giving him food was a way for her to make peace with him. On occasion she even gave some of the food to others in need.

Susan was pleased to see a generous disposition in Emma. But it was clear that at some point further conversation about the equitable distribution of the garden's food needed to happen. As that day's conversation continued, it became plain to Susan that Emma was suffering and embarrassed by her own admission of guilt. What had been a calm conversation suddenly turned to rage on Emma's part as she screamed at Susan, trying to cover her shame with a torrent of hurtful and violent words.

Susan listened to Emma's verbal abuse for an hour. Susan will tell you it was by the grace of God that she neither retaliated nor retreated. She simply sat with her, absorbing her painful outburst, taking in the rage at life that was bottled up inside. Not expecting a quiet, merciful response from Susan, Emma became even angrier. She left the garden in a fury, vowing that the garden would never see her face again.

Several months later Emma called Susan on the phone. Having received a flyer from The Lord's Acre in the mail—a flyer stating that the mission of the garden was to feed poor and hungry people—she said that she now understood her thievery to be wrong and a violation of the work and needs of others. She wanted to apologize. Susan asked if it would be okay for garden members to come to her home and build her a garden, one that included a melon patch. Overwhelmed with tears, Emma expressed how wonderful that would be. Weeks later, no longer screaming in a rage, Emma wrote on the garden chalkboard, "I am *so* blessed. Oh yeah, and happy!"

Emma now comes to The Lord's Acre not to steal but to harvest beans for the local food pantry. She marvels at neighbors who come by her garden to talk about gardening. She reads seed catalogues and is planning what she will plant next year. When she sees Susan, she often asks, "How did we get here from where we started?" Attending to Emma's story, we realize that she could not have arrived where she is without the love The Lord's Acre attempts to embody. As long as Emma was alone and isolated, she could not thrive. She needed the support of a community of people who could feed and nurture and inspire her. She needed the garden to let her know *where* she is (a place of interdependent need and help), *who* she is (a valuable member of a community), and *what* is appropriate for her to do (to be a contributing, harmonious presence among others).

Thinking about Emma and the relationships she has developed helps us see how gardens are places where profound encounters can occur. These encounters with soil, plants, animals, and other people teach us about the many needs we have, needs for nurture and companionship, but also joy and hope. When these encounters happen in the contexts of love and good work, the lives of neighbors, strangers, animals, plants, and land can be woven together into a strong, beautiful fabric that supports community. Of Emma Susan says, "So Emma was hungry for food. That much was obvious. But her deeper hungers—to be loved and heard and valued—could never be found in a box of produce or in a watermelon patch. They could only be found in community, weaving itself in and around Emma, and Emma weaving herself in and through community."[1]

The story of Emma shows us that companionship and community are among a garden's most important crops. *Creation garden style means that life is made for companionship and community.* A community is not simply a *collection* of individuals, but a *membership* of creatures woven together by the daily work of love. When love is present and active, a diverse group of creatures can come together to make a vibrant and healthy whole that, in its wholeness, also assures the thriving of each individual. Being attentive to those present and then lending a helping hand to provide for each member's nurture make it possible for beautiful blooms of all kinds to emerge. Susan is clear: "The Lord's Acre is a food garden, but most people who come to work here say they come because it is beautiful. And that's a result of gardening in community. Each of us on our own couldn't have a garden this lovely. But working together we can." Beauty is the sign that life is thriving and is being celebrated and cared for.

But community is not easy, especially if we include soil, water, plants, and animals in the community's membership. Each of those has needs and potential that are unique, and it takes time, patience, and skill to learn how to nurture them. It would be a crucial error, for instance, to mistake a person for a potato! All who come to the garden come with hungers, wounds, and desires that make the work of weaving difficult, and sometimes very painful. For gardens and communities to thrive, the people in them need appropriate sympathies and detailed understanding. If gardeners are not knowledgeable and careful they will produce suffering rather than beauty. For the weaving together of life to go well, patience, mercy, and forgiveness need to be present.

As Susan sees it, the work she does in the garden is successful not only with regard to the amount of food grown and distributed. The real work, the most important task, is to better involve people in each other's lives, enable them to see how they can be a help to each other, and then invite God's love to take root and grow between them. Good gardening work is about helping people learn to love each other and their homes. Good food is a physical manifestation of the prayer that all creatures be well. But ultimately, the work and the food are not primarily about us. They are about tapping into the divine love that is the animating and sustaining source of every living thing. They are about welcoming God's "lavish, over-the-top love" into our presence and then sharing it with others.

Growing a Garden

IT IS IMPOSSIBLE TO summarize neatly all that a garden is or predict all that a garden will be. Gardens are places with the power to create sympathies and relationships that join people to land, plants, animals, each other, and God. Because each creature and each place are unique, having their own particular needs and potential, it is impossible to know the precise forms these relationships will take. The Lord's Acre, however, is guided by three primary goals. First, the garden exists to provide healthy and nutritious food for people in the community who do not have enough to eat. Second, the garden seeks to create community by bringing people together to work, make music, dance, and share food at a table. And third, the garden serves as an education center teaching its members the art of growing organic food, taking care of the land, and sustaining life together. To grow a garden, people need practical skills in the areas of seed selection, planting, weeding, and soil care, but they also need to cultivate a spirit of humility, gratitude, generosity, and celebration. A loving humanity is a garden's most important crop.

The inspiration and vision for The Lord's Acre came from James G. McClure, a Presbyterian minister from Chicago, who came to North Carolina in the 1930s with a dream to revitalize farming communities. McClure started a farmers' cooperative to help farmers get better prices for what they grew. But he also believed that it is not enough simply to make a living. It is crucial to a community's well-being that people give back and in their giving contribute to the health and resilience of an entire region. People need to have a way to affirm and live out the truth that we do not succeed alone or solely by our own power. For communities to thrive, a spirit of generosity needs to be cultivated.

And so the idea for the original Lord's Acre was born: farmers committed to grow an extra acre of crops or raise an extra animal that would be given to the poor as an expression of their gratitude and devotion to the Lord. Though begun during the Depression, hundreds of farmers and churches, both nationally and internationally, supported the idea, giving a modern expression to the old biblical idea of the tithe, in which people gave back to God one-tenth of what they had received.

To McClure and his followers it was clear that farmers and gardeners occupy a unique place in the world, because they are, by virtue of working with soil and plants and animals, in daily and immediate contact with powers of fertility, birth, growth, and death. They know, with the intimacy of their hands, stomachs, and tongues, that life is a precious and vulnerable gift that cannot be *commandeered,* but must finally be *received.* A good harvest is never to be taken for granted. Growing food in conditions of blight, disease, bad weather, and death compels gardeners to come to terms with their own ignorance and impotence. Gardening teaches them a crucial insight: that individual people cannot thrive on their own, but only by the grace of one another's help. It is an insight no society can long live without.

McClure's dream of resilient farming communities was a powerful one, prompting Henry Wallace, in 1935 the Secretary of Agriculture, to come to North Carolina and proclaim, "Great spiritual power will eventually emanate from these mountains of western North Carolina. . . ." Wallace had seen that a capitalist, strictly market logic encouraged people to perceive the world as a storehouse of limitless commodities that were there to be taken and profited from. But what could be more naive and damaging than to think that people can simply purchase their way through life, oblivious to the limits and the responsibilities of appropriate consumption? He placed great hope in The Lord's Acre project, because it represented a vision founded upon communal work and the receiving and sharing of gifts, a vision that acknowledged our fundamental needs and our calling to be a source of help and nurture to one another.

As World War II came to an end, so did the work of The Lord's Acre. Rather than rely on each other and God's provision, people put their hope in markets, industrial production methods, insurance programs, and government subsidies. The exodus of farmers to cities, the growth of a prosperous middle class, and the proliferation of consumer products trained people to think they didn't need each other, that they could make it on their own.

The story of the birth of The Lord's Acre demonstrates that people can plan their ambition and goals according to vastly different moral maps. A map that directs people to stores as the primary destination, for instance, is vastly different from a map that directs people to gardens. Depending on the map that is your guide, you will be encouraged and expected to behave in significantly different ways. Multiple maps exist, and the maps by which people direct their lives change. We need to think carefully about where our maps are coming from and if they are taking us to destinations that are good and worthy of our effort.

By 2009 it was clear to residents in Fairview, North Carolina, that McClure's vision needed to be revived. The industrial methods of food production and the capitalist logic that Wallace decried had left many people poor, isolated, and in desperate need of good food. Food insecurity, even in communities located in rich agricultural lands, had become a national problem. Clearly there was something wrong with the modern capitalist industrial map, because it was taking people to places that left them hungry and alone. And so the new The Lord's Acre was born with the following mission: "The

Lord's Acre is a diverse and open community of volunteers who grow and give away organic food. Using the garden as a platform, The Lord's Acre is a visionary model of cooperation which educates and inspires people to address the many types of hunger through caring service and the growing and sharing of food."

In its first year the garden produced on a quarter of an acre 3 tons of fresh food that went to Food for Fairview, a local pantry. In 2012 it grew 9 tons on three-quarters of an acre, supplying every kind of vegetable and fruit imaginable to the pantry, to Veteran's Restoration Quarters in Asheville, and to the Fairview Welcome Table, a local establishment that prepares a weekly fresh-food "pay what you can, if you can" meal to anyone who wants to come and eat.

That good food is produced clearly matters, because food is the material expression of God's desire that all creatures be cared for. But what is most important is the calling down and then cultivation of the divine love that keeps the garden going and gives it a purpose. Susan says, "Whenever I look for a deeper *why,* I always find the gospel, God's lavish, over-the-top love. And if this love is flowing all over the place, it has to go somewhere. So when my *why* changes from something I can do and feel good about and becomes something God did and I just have to share it, it changes absolutely everything."

The Lord's Acre depends on volunteers and the generous support of community members. It is building partnerships with community groups, area schools, and Warren Wilson College. It is bringing together children, adults, and seniors, so that intergenerational understanding can develop. Speaking for the garden, Susan says their collective aim is to put the garden out of business. She dreams of a time when the institution is no longer needed, because unlike an organization that exists to perpetuate itself, The Lord's Acre longs for the day when everyone naturally knows and spontaneously practices the growing and sharing of food and the weaving and the strengthening of communal memberships. Then all our dwelling places will be garden communities that are beautiful and that create the occasions for us to get to know and cherish one another. People will have maps that enable them to move deeply into the places and communities of their life and be a nurturing presence there.

This is a big vision for such a small plot of land. But if you ask Susan, she will tell you that the hope of the world depends on places like it, places where people learn to love each other, love the earth, and in so doing give physical expression to their love for God as the Source of life. The Lord's Acre does many things, but according to Susan, "What we really do is make love visible. It is a profound calling to look at whatever is before us and ask, 'How can I make love visible here and now?'"

Making love visible! This is the essential mission of The Lord's Acre. It is also the most fundamental meaning of every garden. Love is much more than a good feeling or emotion. It is the discipline and power that welcomes and nurtures life and helps it flourish. To practice love requires considerably more than simply "being nice." It takes sympathy, knowledge, and practical skill to meet another's need. Love is the daily and difficult work of moving toward what scripture calls *shalom*. Borrowing from the work of Timothy Keller, Susan describes shalom this way:

> Shalom is so much more than "peace." It is complete flourishing and reconciliation in all relationships. God turned a chaos into cosmos, and also turned a tangle into a tapestry. This fabric metaphor conveys the importance of relationship. If you throw thousands of pieces of thread onto a table, no fabric results. The threads must be rightly and intimately related to one another in literally a million ways. Each thread must go over, under, around, and through the others at thousands of points. Only then do you get a fabric that is beautiful and strong, that covers, fits, holds, shelters, and delights. This interwovenness and flourishing is shalom.

At The Lord's Acre each garden member is asked to become a thread within a tapestry that interweaves earthworms, butterflies, water, sunflowers, melons, Emma, homeless veterans, and whoever happens to show up. God is not a thread within the tapestry. Instead, God is the Weaver—the power of love—that moves among and within the threads. Because love is not merely a pious or emotional sentiment, it requires each garden member to ask practical questions like, "What do these plants need to thrive?" or "What does Emma need to be well?" or "What do the soil, the beneficial insects, and the honeybees need in order to flourish—not individually, but in their connectedness?" and then respond with skillful work. When all this happens, the performance of *making love visible* is under way. As Susan sees it, God's love is going on all around us all the time. That we exist is the "proof" of that. What God wants is for us to tap into and use the currency of this love, so that everyone can be nurtured and fed.

God's Gardening Way with the World

THE LORD'S ACRE DEMONSTRATES that the meaning of life is found in the receiving, nurturing, and sharing of God's gifts of love. Why? Because life *is* God's love made visible, fragrant, audible, touchable, and nutritious. Life is not a pointless struggle or a random accident. It is God's *creation*. As such, it is the material manifestation of the divine love that delights in the flourishing of others. Of course, life's creatures can be wounded and horribly disfigured. But when life achieves fullness and abundance, when it most clearly realizes its inner truth, it is the unfolding of God's love. It is the full realization of what God always wants creation to be.

The Psalmist describes this vision of creation beautifully. He notes that it is God who establishes the heavens, the waters, the clouds, and the wind. God puts the earth with its mountains and valleys on a secure and reliable foundation. God waters the earth and makes springs gush forth, so that creatures can drink. God causes the growth of plants and food that nourish all abundantly. Indeed, all things look to God for their being and nurture. Rising in a crescendo of marvel and delight, the Psalmist exclaims, "O LORD, how manifold are your works! In wisdom you have made them all; the earth is full of your creatures" (104:24).

Why does God do any of this? Because God delights in newness of life, fecundity, and shining faces and glad hearts. In a remarkable passage we are given the point of view of divine Wisdom, said to be present at the creation of the world. Wisdom is beside God as a witness to all that God is doing when establishing the heavens and forming the mountains. Like a young child, Wisdom is presented as dancing and rejoicing in the splendor of all that is happening. Speaking of God, Wisdom says, "I was beside him, like a master worker; and I was daily his delight, rejoicing before him always, rejoicing in his inhabited world and delighting in the human race" (Prov. 8:30–31). The Knox translation of the Bible captures the sense of delight beautifully: "I made play in this world of dust, with the sons of Adam for my play-fellows." Creation is the effect of God's joy in seeing another creature come into being.

There is not the slightest inkling here of a distant or disinterested God who kick-started a world long ago and now leaves it to itself. God creates out of love and remains with creatures not in order to dominate and control, but to support and sustain them. The God who creates is—like a gardener—fully present to the world and committed to be with it daily, nurturing and leading it into the fullness of life. What the Psalmist most dreads is that God may one day turn away. When that happens, all creation will come to an end:

> These all look to you
>   to give them their food in due season;

when you give to them, they gather it up;

  when you open your hand, they are filled with good things.

When you hide your face, they are dismayed;

  when you take away their breath, they die

  and return to their dust.

When you send forth your spirit [breath], they are created;

  and you renew the face of the ground. (Ps. 104:27–30)

To appreciate the ethos of the Psalmist's vision and its references to God's face and breath directed to dust and ground, we need to consider the oldest biblical story of creation, a story that takes us to another garden, this time the more famous Garden of Eden. The name is important—Eden literally means "delight."

Entering Eden we encounter an astonishing sight. God appears as the First Gardener, with knees on the ground and hands in the soil: "And the Lord God planted a garden in Eden, in the east" (Gen. 2:8). Why did the ancient Israelites choose this way to introduce God to us, especially when surrounding ancient cultures gave us divine beings who create with violent power? Why choose a garden scene to communicate the fundamental structure and orientation of reality?

God does not create from a distance or at arm's length. God creates through intimacy and by offering God's own self to others. God shares God's own breath to bring about the breathing of the world. Being the First Gardener, God holds the soil close and then breathes into it, making the first human being come to shape and to life: *adam* (Adam) from *adamah* (the soil of the earth). But not just human beings. Out of the same ground God creates "every tree that is pleasant to the sight and good for food" (Gen. 2:9) and "every animal of the field and every bird of the air" (2:19). Every living thing moves because it is animated by God's own Spirit, or life-giving breath. The image we are given is of a gardening God who loves soil and who, by giving God's self to it, creates the creatures and the conditions from which further life can follow. God is as near and as intimate as the life within our own breath.

God is not a spectator. God is at the heart of the action, fully present and fully engaged. God *plants* the world, which is to say that God is continually at work making places fertile, beautiful, and fruitful. As the primordial and essential Gardener, God is concerned to create conditions in which new life can sprout and spread, life that will be a source of nurture and a joy to behold. It would be ridiculous to think that as a gardener God would depart when life is coming to fragrant bloom or succulent harvest. In this opening scene we are taught to see creation as a membership of creatures living in interdependent and beneficial relationship with each other. Nothing is alone. Nothing is irrelevant. Whatever exists does so because it contributes to the flowering of life.

It is important to see in this story God's profound pleasure in the world and its creatures. God delights in life's flowering, attending to it as a gardener lingers with individual plants— preparing soil for seed, applying water and compost as needed, trimming excess growth, delighting in beauty. God enjoys the garden and wants to be in it, which is why God is described as one who takes walks in Eden in the cool of the evening breeze (Gen. 3:8). And God wants humanity to enjoy it too. God places the *adam* in the garden with specific instructions: join with me in taking care of it and in doing so share in the work and the delight that a garden provides (2:15). God calls humanity to practical intimacy with creation, because in drawing near to earthworms, bees, and flowers in acts of care, contemplation, and celebration, we also draw near to God's joy there at work.

It is tempting to dismiss this story as a fairy tale. Does anyone really believe the world literally begins as a garden made and maintained by a divine Gardener? Clearly not. But as I already indicated, the point of this story is not to give us a scientific account of how it all began. Its purpose is to communicate something about who

God is and what this world's and this life's significance are. Reading it, we are to understand that we and everything else are creatures that need each other and are utterly dependent upon God for the breath of life that enables us to flourish. We are to understand that everything is a gift cherished by God and meant to be a source of mutual delight. For us to live well, the memberships of creatures that live with us and through us—what Susan Sides describes as the weaving of countless threads—need to be healthy and whole too. That is an ecological and a theological truth. It is a truth that positions each one of us in a place of moral and practical responsibility. Creation is the place where God's love is made visible. The quintessential human task is to harmonize our love with God's own love everywhere at work in the world. This love is no mere abstraction or pious sentiment. It is realized in practical, detailed skills that nurture life into its fullness.

CHAPTER 6

The Feast of Creation:
On Learning Hospitality

We were given appetites, not to consume the world and forget it, but to
taste its goodness and hunger to make it great.
ROBERT FARRAR CAPON.[1]

WHAT SORT OF PLACE is the world, and what is its character? We
rarely stop to ponder these questions, but they are crucial, because
how we answer them goes a long way in determining how we are
going to live in it. For instance, if I believe that the world is one big
store or warehouse, a stockpile of "natural resources," then I will
think of myself primarily as a consumer who lives by shopping. The
things of this world exist to be purchased and owned. The point of
industry is to make them available as widely, cheaply, and efficiently
as possible. And the key to a successful human life is to have enough
money to maximize my purchasing power.

But why think of the world this way? I have already suggested that another way to characterize this world is as a garden. Understood this way, places and creatures (humans included) are fragile and vulnerable, susceptible to powers of fertility and decay, flourishing and death. In gardens people learn that all life is shaped by need—the need for nurture, protection, and inspiration. The key to a successful human life is not to maximize purchasing power, but to develop and refine the gardening skills that best nurture, protect, and celebrate the *gifts,* rather than the *commodities,* of life. The point is not, first and foremost, to take, but to learn to attend to and receive. Shoppers and gardeners, though both reside on planet earth, live in fundamentally different worlds. The doctrine of creation helps us clarify the character of the world as the embodiment of God's love and thus gives us practical insights on how best to live where we are.

In this chapter creation is characterized as a feast in which the love of God is made available for all to enjoy. Things do not simply exist in some rudimentary or boring way. They are alive with vibrant colors, intoxicating aromas, and delectable flavors. Should we not be astounded by the sight of an iris, the fragrance of a lilac, and the taste of a ripe raspberry? Granted, there is plenty of pain and suffering in the world to make us aware that alongside beauty there is also ugliness. But we would be supremely inattentive and ungrateful if we failed to notice and appreciate the sensory wonders of this world. The world is a place of splendor (from the Latin *splendere,* "to shine, be bright"), because the love of God shines through it.

The divine love that creates a feast is a love that "makes room" for others to be. It is a love that opens a space of freedom and possibility in which creatures can be welcomed, nurtured, and then empowered to explore all the potential that is uniquely theirs. At its best, life is not a drag or an ordeal, but an invitation to experience diversity and fullness. Why? Because the love that creates is ultimately hospitable. From a Christian point of view, it makes good sense to describe creation as a lavish and complex act of divine *hospitality*. God, in addition to being the First and Essential Gardener, is also the supreme and generous Host. God desires nothing more than for creatures to delight in the goodness and beauty of all that has been created. God wants people to learn to share in this hospitable work by nurturing and encouraging others into the fullness of their lives.

But this is not easily done. For a variety of reasons, we often find it difficult to be guests at the feast and to receive gratefully the generosity that has been given. Are we worried that we are diminished by the splendor of another's presence? And we often find it hard to be generous hosts, committed to putting our energy and attention in service of another's well-being. Are we worried that we will be left behind or unappreciated?

To help us think through these matters, we can turn to another foundational biblical story, the story of Noah and the ark, because in it we find important insight into what it means for people to be creatures participating in God's nurturing and hospitable ways with the world. Noah's service on the ark fulfills humanity's vocation to work for the flourishing of creatures. Noah is a model of faithful living, because he is willing to be shaped and directed by the love of God, which is hospitable at its core.

Returning to the book of Genesis, we see that it does not take long for violence to enter the Garden of Eden. What began as a place of delight is disturbed by arrogance, anxiety, and murder. Adam and Eve eat the forbidden fruit. Their son Cain kills his brother, Abel. Having forsaken the responsibility of caring for creatures, humanity now finds itself banished from the garden. This new condition of exile and loss grieves God to the heart: "The LORD saw that the wickedness of humankind was great in the earth, and that every inclination of the thoughts of their hearts was only evil continually.

And the LORD was sorry that he had made humankind on the earth, and it grieved him to his heart" (6:5–6).

It is hard to imagine the divine pathos revealed in this passage. What began as God's delight in a world beautifully and delectably made has moved into God's sorrow and utter disappointment. God resolves to "blot out" all creatures in an act of de-creation: rather than breathing soil to life, God will release a deluge of water that will turn the soil into one vast sea of mud.

Among humanity, however, there is one man, Noah, who found favor with God. We are told that he was righteous and "walked with God" (Gen. 6:9), suggesting that he lived in ways that were faithful to God's life-giving presence in the world. Noah and his family are going to be spared from the flood's destruction. They are going to build an ark that will house and nurture the creatures of the world, thereby demonstrating what it means to be hospitable, as God is.

It is tempting to interpret the ark as a rescue vehicle. In this reading Noah gathers seed stock and species specimens to repopulate the earth once the flood is over. But what if something much more important is going on, something showing us what it means to be a creature living in God's creation? What if the ark is not an escape vessel, but a school for the learning of compassion and delight? And what if the work Noah is about to do is an apprenticeship in the ways of God's love?

Noah's building of the ark is an outrageous act. God tells Noah that the whole earth is about to be destroyed and then instructs him to build the ark, bring on board two of every kind of living flesh, and make provisions for all the food necessary for creatures to survive. Noah is successful. But to be successful he had to have a deep appreciation for the splendor of creatures. He had to love them by studying them, learning their ways, and discerning their needs. Otherwise he could not have been their host. The flood comes and destroys everything, but the ark and all its creatures are safe. Noah emerges from the ark "a man of the soil" (Gen. 9:20), an *adam* responsive to the needs of *adamah*. Noah warrants this description because he performs what the first and subsequent generations of humanity failed to do: take care of the soil and all the creatures that depend on it.

Noah's deep significance is that his love for the creatures was a witness to God's primordial, creative hospitality. Imagine the kind of knowledge and sympathy Noah must have possessed to determine which creatures should be brought on board. Imagine too the devotion and skill he must have displayed to feed and nurture these creatures the many months they are reported to have stayed in the ark. As one rabbinic tradition suggested, Noah so enjoyed his role as host that he never stopped to sleep. To sleep would have been to miss out on the opportunity and joy that comes from seeing guests well nurtured and celebrated!

What the story of Noah shows is that the world exists only through the action of hospitality, most basically God's own hospitality in founding and sustaining the world, but then also our own hospitality as we work with God to be a nurturing and celebrating presence to others. To be hospitable is not to seek benefits or glory for ourselves. It is instead to develop the sympathy capable of inviting into our life creatures often vastly different from us and then to affirm them in their difference. It is to give ourselves to others by learning the specific skills—like "home" (rather than merely "house") construction, food production and preparation, conflict mediation—that equip us to address the need and potential unique to each guest. And it is to demonstrate the humility, kindness, and generosity that position us to serve the many needs we share with each other.

All of us, simply by being who we are, are the beneficiaries of hospitality. We live by the gifts of friendship, instruction, and support that others give to us. But not everyone perceives and appreciates it or acts accordingly. When the world is understood as the place of God's primordial, ongoing hospitality—something that gardens and the work of gardening are uniquely suited to help us do—then it becomes apparent that people made "in the image of God" are called, like Noah, to be the hosts that welcome, nurture, and celebrate others.

A Story of Transformed Perception

As I HAVE BEEN stressing in this part of the book, to perceive the world and its life *as creation* is to say something about the significance of all that is and the character of the relationships that hold all things together. It is to affirm that nothing exists by itself, from itself, or for itself. Being is relational and communal. It is also completely gratuitous. Nothing has to be. That anything exists at all is only because of a divine love that sees existence as mutual thriving as good. Things hold together and do not fall apart because the reconciling love witnessed in the life of Jesus is circulating through everything. It is God facing the world, breathing on everything and thereby animating it from within, and exercising the divine hospitality that enlivens creatures and keeps them on the move.

The difficulty, but also the beauty, of learning to perceive creation in this way is shown in *Babette's Feast,* a short story written by Isak Dinesen and then made into a movie under the direction of Gabriel Axel. The story takes place in the tiny Norwegian town of Berlevaag. This town is home to a small, pious sect founded by a prophet who had two beautiful daughters, Martine and Philippa. People from all around Norway looked up to this group. "Its members renounced the pleasures of this world, for the earth and all that it held to them was but a kind of illusion, and the true reality was the New Jerusalem toward which they were longing."[2] Dinesen writes that for this congregation, "earthly love, and marriage with it, were trivial matters, in themselves nothing but illusions. . . . The fair girls had been brought up to an ideal of heavenly love; they were all filled with it and did not let themselves be touched by the flames of this world." The members of this Christian sect lived an austere, though not unkind life. The daughters were both known for their works of charity and their welcome of those who had need.

One rainy night Babette Hersant comes to their door, nearly dead from exhaustion and distress. She has come from Paris, where she had found herself to be on the wrong side of a civil war. Though Martine and Philippa do not need and cannot afford an experienced housekeeper, Babette begs to stay. She vows to work for nothing.

Babette soon sees that she has entered a vastly different world in this Norwegian town, a world in which people had lost a sense of the splendor of God's creation. Once a famous chef in Paris (a fact that does not register with the daughters) and thus one who delighted in the world's delectability, Babette is now asked to prepare the plainest of food: split cod and ale-and-bread soup. "The first day after Babette had entered their service, they took her before them and explained to her that they were poor and that to them luxurious fare was sinful. Their own food must be as plain as possible; it was the soup-pails and baskets for their poor that signified." Babette took to her new life in earnest, bringing excellence and efficiency to her management of the household.

One day the daughters decide to celebrate the one-hundredth anniversary of their father's birth. The small community of his followers had fallen into discord and petty sniping at each other. The daughters' hope was that an occasion marking the spiritual aspirations of their father might heal age-old resentments and bring the community back together again. Weeks before the anniversary date, Babette receives a letter from France announcing that she has won 10,000 francs in a lottery. She begs Martina and Philippa to let her make a grand dinner for the anniversary and pay for it herself. She wants to make the dinner an expression of prayer. What better way to celebrate the life of a man than to celebrate the love that makes possible the wonder of delectable food? The daughters do not like the idea, but they can find no good way to refuse Babette's request.

To make preparation for the dinner, Babette returns to Paris—the ingredients needed for a feast could hardly be found in Berlevaag. She returns with fine wine, a live turtle, and all kinds of delicacies that had never touched Martine's or Philippa's tongues. The daughters are clearly worried by this lavish, worldly display of food. They go to various members of their community to offer a warning. Together they make a promise: "They would, on the great day, be silent upon all matters of food and drink. Nothing that might be set before them, be it even frog or snails, should wring a word from their lips."

The members of this little community, devout as they are, are clearly worried that they will be tempted by the aromas and flavors of the food. They are afraid that they might enjoy what they eat and drink and in their enjoyment forsake God (mistakenly assuming that one cannot at the same time enjoy God and what God has made). This is why one of the old men says, "On the day of our master we will cleanse our tongues of all taste and purify them of all delight or disgust of the senses, keeping and preserving them for the higher things of praise and thanksgiving."

Among the dinner guests is General Loewenhielm, a distinguished army officer who had been to Berlevaag many years before as a young man and then fallen in love with Martine. Because Martine was unable to return his love, Loewenhielm departed a despondent man. Turning dejection into ambition, he quickly climbed the ladder of success. He "had obtained everything that he had striven for in life and was admired and envied by everyone." But on his trip to Babette's dinner party, he felt a strange sadness. Perhaps all his achievements were little more than an exercise in vanity. In gaining the whole world, had he lost his soul?

With dinner prepared and the table set, the guests arrive and are seated. A table grace is offered: "May my food my body maintain, may my body my soul sustain, may my soul in deed and word give thanks for all things to the Lord." But at the word "food" the members of the congregation remember their vow: they promised not to give the food the slightest attention or thought. They eat and drink with a grave countenance. They eat no differently than if their plates were filled with split cod and ale-and-bread soup, oblivious to the fact that they are seated at a feast.

All except the general. Having dined with some of the most influential and wealthy people in Europe, General Loewenhielm knows that he is drinking only the very best wine and eating food that in its quality exceeds that at the finest restaurants in France. Not knowing that Babette is the cook, he is astounded that food in this town can taste this good. Upon tasting the main dish, Cailles en Sarcophage, he is overcome and pronounces that this dish was invented by "the greatest culinary genius of the age," a woman who had managed to turn eating "into a kind of love affair . . . in which one no longer distinguishes between bodily and spiritual appetite or satiety!"

As the meal progresses it is clear that the mood of the congregation is improving, but there is little speaking. The general, however, feels it is time to make a speech. Though normally in complete control of what he wants to say, this time he finds himself to be a mouthpiece for words he could not have prepared. He says:

> We have all of us been told that grace is to be found in the
> universe. But in our human foolishness and short-sightedness
> we imagine divine grace to be finite. For this reason we
> tremble. . . . But the moment comes when our eyes are opened,
> and we see and realize that grace is infinite. Grace, my friends,
> demands nothing from us but that we shall await it with
> confidence and acknowledge it in gratitude. . . . Grace takes
> us all to its bosom and proclaims general amnesty. See! That

which we have chosen is given us, and that which we have refused is, also and at the same time, granted us. Ay, that which we have rejected is poured upon us abundantly. For mercy and truth have met together, and righteousness and bliss have kissed one another!

The congregation members seated at the table do not understand this speech, nor do they later remember it. They didn't need to. Dinesen describes the room as filled with a heavenly light, "as if a number of small halos had blended into one glorious radiance. Taciturn old people received the gift of tongues; ears that for years had been almost deaf were opened to it. Time itself merged into eternity." Before the members went out into the night, the grievances that had kept them apart from each other were forgiven. Dinesen observes:

When later in life they thought of this evening it never occurred to any of them that they might have been exalted by their own merit. They realized that the infinite grace of which General Loewenhielm had spoken had been allotted to them, and they did not even wonder at the fact, for it had been but the fulfillment of an ever-present hope. The vain illusions of this earth had dissolved before their eyes like smoke, and they had seen the universe as it really is. They had been given one hour of the millennium.

For the people in this tiny village, the map of the world had been changed, because they experienced at table together the hospitable love that moves the universe into life.

Babette's feast was clearly a transformative moment in the lives of this little congregation. It enabled its members to see each other in a nonquarrelsome and forgiving way. One could say that their eating together was the occasion in which they perceived the world as a gracious gift and a gratuitous, unnecessary act of love. Being witnesses to such love, tasting it with their tongues, transformed them so that they could be inspired to live with each other in more forgiving, generous, and hospitable ways.

Tasting Creation

TO APPRECIATE THE POWER of a cooked meal and the significance of Babette's creative effort, we can read this story alongside the insights of Robert Farrar Capon, an Episcopal priest and chef. Capon observes that few of us have learned the skill of paying attention. We don't take much time to notice, let alone appreciate, the many miracles of novelty, variety, and taste that surround us. He says, "Man's real work is to look at the things of this world and to love them for what they are. That is, after all, what God does, and man was not made in God's image for nothing."[3] The worst human fate imaginable would be boredom, because boredom means that a person no longer finds the world to be compelling or lovely enough to warrant attention.

As a "culinary genius" Babette had learned the art of attention. She had looked out upon the world and found it to be a delectable place capable of releasing flavors and fragrances that can delight the nose and the tongue. Dinesen does not provide much information as to Babette's theological sensitivities, but as Capon sees it, "Food is the daily sacrament of unnecessary goodness, ordained for a continual remembrance that the world will always be more delicious than it is useful."[4] Babette must have had an inkling about this because she spent, much to the daughters' horror, the entire 10,000 francs on this meal. The point of life, apparently, is not to reduce it to its usefulness. More important than any pragmatic consideration is the question of whether we have the capacity to be amazed by a world that has so much potential to taste so good and then to share that amazement with others.

The general clearly was amazed by and appreciative of what he was eating. Reading Capon, one can readily imagine Loewenhielm offering Capon's toast:

> **To a radically, perpetually unnecessary world; to the restoration of astonishment to the heart and mystery to the mind; to wine, because it is a gift we never expected; to mushroom and artichoke, for they are incredible legacies; to improbable acids and high alcohols, since we would hardly have thought of them ourselves; and to all being, because it is superfluous. . . . *Cheers,* Men and Brethren. We are free: nothing is needful, everything is for joy. Let the bookkeepers struggle with their balance sheets; it is the tippler who sees the untipped Hand. God is eccentric; He has *love,* not reasons. Salute!**[5]

To live in a world of grace that is infinite means that the world as created is good. The goodness of things does not depend on how they contribute or fail to contribute to somebody's chosen end, but is simply a feature of their being themselves. This is what creation *ex amore* means.

The Norwegian congregation had difficulty living in reconciled and joyful relationship with each other because they had assumed that "the earth and all that it held to them was but a kind of illusion." Though they showed compassion and hospitality from time to time, their love could not find a more complete expression, because their starting assumption was that materiality was an impediment to the love of God, rather than a physical manifestation of it. Committed to an ideal of "heavenly love," they did not appreciate how the love of creatures in their earthy materiality could be a participation in the divine love that delights in creaturely goodness. To deny the eternal worth of material creation must eventually result in a denial of the eternal worth of human bodies and thus a forgetting of Jesus's embodiment and his promise that bodies will be resurrected to be with God forever.

The doctrine of creation teaches that creaturely life achieves its fulfillment not in the disdain, but in the delight of the world. Here it is important to recall that the Bible begins with a seven-day creation poem in which God regularly sees and pronounces that what is made is good. The poem does not end on the sixth day with the creation of humanity, as though humanity was the climax of it all. It ends on the seventh day with God observing *shabbat,* because Sabbath observance marks the climax and fulfillment of creation. Here we see that *the trajectory of the logic of God's love is to end in delighting in the goodness of the creatures that love creates.*

On the first Sabbath God beholds the goodness and beauty of everything as the sensory expression of his own love. During this Sabbath time God does not flee or long to escape from the world. Instead, God becomes fully present and delights in the splendor of creatures that have the potential to be beautiful, fragrant, and delectable. God then instructs human beings to observe the Sabbath and in doing so share in the delight that brought into being and still today sustains the world.

To practice Sabbath is to rest. More exactly, it is to participate in God's resting in the world. It is easy to be mistaken about what this rest is and what it entails. Many of us, for instance, crave rest because we are exhausted from all the busyness and the frantic pace of daily life. Life is hard, perhaps even a burden, and so we long for escape.

But Sabbath is not about escaping from the world. God is not exhausted by this world. What God attends to on the first Sabbath sunrise is a world that reflects God's own goodness and love. And so rather than wanting to escape from the world, what God's resting does is highlight the splendor of life and celebrate all the beauty that makes this world a place of delight. Narrated this way, Sabbath rest is not about stopping, but about exchanging our restlessness for delight. Restlessness, which can also be defined as impatience and ingratitude, is the problem. When we are not attentive to and satisfied with things, our stance in life becomes contentious and wearisome.

The goal of life is to learn to delight in the love that shines all around us. It is to slow down and take the time to be amazed by the delicacy of things and discover why each creature needs cherishing. And when we perceive that love is being frustrated in others, our task is to commit, like a host, to their welcome, nurture, and empowerment, so that they can again be the splendid creatures that they are.

When people prepare and share a meal in a mindful, grateful manner, they have the opportunity to witness to God's delight in the world and in doing that invite others to perceive God's world as a lavish feast. We are always welcome guests. But, made in the image of God, we are also called to extend God's hospitable love to others. Joy had departed from the community at Berlevaag, because its members had come to gauge each other by their usefulness. They did not receive each other as gifts, but as competitors who slandered or cheated or undermined each other. And so a somber, gray mood had settled upon this tiny town. What they lacked was a sense of the gratuitous splendor of being and an understanding that life exists as the medium of love and delight.

Babette's feast had so much transformative power because "real eating will restore the festivity of being. Food does not exist merely for the sake of its nutritional value. To see it so is only . . . to regard not what things are, but what they mean to us—to become, in short, solemn idolaters spiritualizing what should be loved as matter."[6] Though members of the congregation vowed not to let the taste of the food inspire comment, its delectable flavor overwhelmed them and slowly and silently brought a convivial atmosphere to the room. Babette's preparation of the food was a tangible, tasty expression of her love for her guests and a witness to the primordial, hospitable love that first created and daily sustains the whole universe. Her love was presented and released into her community to act like a seasoning salt that could enliven and render more enjoyable their life together.

PART III

Fall

CHAPTER 7

When Love Fails, Life Falls Apart

My joy is gone, grief is upon me, my heart is sick.
JEREMIAH 8:18

IF LOVE IS THE power that creates and weaves the creatures of this world into a thriving and beautiful whole—what previous chapters described as a verdant garden, a flourishing community, and a delectable feast—then love's distortion or denial inevitably leads to the unraveling and degradation of life. When love fails or goes awry, creatures are frustrated in their ability to fully become themselves, and they are unable to contribute to the well-being of others. The whole world suffers and slowly falls apart.

In this third part of the book we now consider the ways in which love is distorted and denied. Though love is a beautiful thing, its misunderstanding and misappropriation can quickly make life and this world ugly. But how does misunderstanding set in? What are the conditions that prompt love's degradation? These matters are not obvious or readily apparent, which is why Christians have found it important to analyze carefully the dynamics and dimensions of love's perversion. Each of the three chapters in this part will, therefore, give us some insight into the various dimensions of love's failure.

When Christians talk about the degradation of the world, they often describe it as a "fall" from divine grace. Though life was created by God as good and beautiful, made to be nurtured and celebrated, human beings became sinful and thus brought about needless suffering and misery, which now affects the whole world. Sin is the twisted and misdirected power that causes creatures to stumble and come to grief. By turning people *away* from God, sin is also the force that turns them *against* life.

Sin, at its core, is the *failure* of love. It isn't simply the absence of love, because if love were completely absent, nothing could be. It makes more sense to speak of this failure as a corruption of love and as a perversion of the power that otherwise animates creatures into life. Having turned away from God or finding themselves unable to approach God, people cannot participate in or extend to others the hospitable love that facilitates life's flourishing. Sinners thus find themselves misappropriating and misusing the creative, life-giving power of God by turning it into a power that de-creates and deforms others. If love is what guides people in the ways of nurture, celebration, and peace, sin puts people on paths that lead to loneliness, exploitation, and conflict.

Sin isn't simply a bad decision or a wicked mentality, though it can certainly take these forms. Besides being a personal disposition, it is also a presence or a power that has the effect of rendering people unable to love. The apostle Paul went so far as to describe it as a cosmic power aligned with the devil that produces evil and destruction (Eph. 6:12). Sin is a disabling force that locks people in prisons of fear, anxiety, and darkness, so that they cannot relate to others or themselves in nurturing and celebratory ways. Sin is the failure of love, and people caught in its grip find themselves unable to live fully. People fail to love not only because they are too wrapped up in their own ambition; sometimes they fail to love because they are consumed by their own fear, insecurity, and worry.

If love is the optic that enables people to recognize in each other the gracious and precious character of life, then sin is a form of blindness that causes people to misperceive and mistake the world. It is a mode of being that results in the disintegration of relationships because people don't know how to relate to each other properly. Rather than meeting others in their God-given loveliness, sinful beings tend to relate to others in modes of domination or boredom or neglect.

The story of sin is not simply the depressingly long recounting of the many acts of depravity that punctuate our histories. It is, rather, the distorted narrative that causes us to see everything— even God—in a depraved way. Having rejected love or, perhaps more accurately, having decided to accept diminished and distorted forms of love that meet certain limiting conditions—"I will love you *if* . . ."—we tend to see fellow creatures as threats or competitors and God as a tyrant or a bully.

Sin, in other words, has the effect of placing people in a perpetual state of disorder and corruption. The disorder is so pervasive that the people trapped within it are unable to detect it. Caught in the midst of corruption, people cannot see disorder for what it really is. It can only appear as normal. What is lost is the ability to see how perverted forms of love lead to a fundamental confusion about life—why life matters, what it is for, and how it is best realized—and a basic misunderstanding about God. Having become corrupted, we will inevitably do damage to ourselves, others, and the world around. Think of how much people have been hurt by the image of a vindictive God poised and happy to punish and inflict pain. This is not the God of love. This is the vengeful God of a sick heart that cannot see past its own sinful nature.

The distortion I am talking about isn't simply mental or intellectual. If it was, then living beautifully would be a matter of having more information or better computational skill. These we clearly have in abundance. In fact, never before in human history have we had more education, data, and technique at our fingertips. As good as these may be, however, they are not enough, because it is also the case that never before have we seen more damage being done to the earth and to its various communities.

The corruption that degrades and destroys life goes much deeper than the brain, having its source within us at the place scripture calls the heart. The heart isn't simply the physical organ that pumps blood. It is the spiritual center of our being, the place that determines what we care about and what motivates and excites us. The heart is the place that shapes and drives our feelings and desires, often in ways that are unknown to us. It is what inspires our thinking, speaking, and doing. Understood spiritually, the heart is the organ that animates and directs where our life as a whole goes. A heart consumed by fear and insecurity will, for instance, result in a life vastly different from a heart inspired by compassion and mercy. This is why the Psalmist pleads with God, "Create in me a clean heart, O God, and put a new and right spirit within me" (Ps. 51:10). He knows that an enduring change of life requires a change of heart. He knows that if his heart is not right, all his living will be off too.

Love's distortion is not a choice between loving or not. It is, rather, about attempting forms of love that are diseased rather than healthy, dirty rather than clean, degrading rather than nurturing. When the heart is sick—as when it becomes infected by anxiety or revenge or arrogance—people can *think* they are acting out of love, but in truth are really living out a fantasy of power or control. To see what I mean, think of the number of people who abuse their spouses or children while claiming to love them.

Love's denial has its roots in a heart that is diseased. This disease, to be sure, will result in bad decisions. But even more important, one's entire way of perceiving and being in the world will become clouded, negligent, or injurious. When people are muddled about love, they gradually lose the *sympathies* to recognize each other's need and pain, the *imagination* to envision each other's flourishing, the *commitment* to work patiently with others to help them realize their potential, and the *joy* that cherishes and celebrates the goodness that others are. In other words, corrupted love results in a distorted map, which results in a misdirected way of life.

Love is the lens that brings the world into proper focus, enabling persons to perceive and receive each other as precious yet vulnerable gifts. When we love another properly, the uniqueness of that person's being, the things that make that person special, can come into view and be respected. But to have a good lens you need to have a clean heart, one that welcomes and appreciates others in their God-given goodness. You need to stop perceiving others as what you wish them to be (perhaps because they will then fulfill the plans that suit you). When people are mistaken about what love is and what it requires, they lose the ability to properly care for themselves, their communities, and the places in which they live. They don't really appreciate where they are or who they are with. As a result, they don't know how faithfully to "be" where they are.

The Grip of Sin

FOR THE MOST PART, people do not choose to be sick and corrupt. Owing to any number of environmental, social, and personal factors, people are slowly and often imperceptibly conditioned into it. The great tragedy of love's perversion is that people can be in it and not even know it. Not knowing it, they lash out in desperate and destructive fits that only exacerbate each other's pain and loneliness. To see what I mean, we can take a brief look at the Weston family as presented in *August: Osage County,* the Pulitzer Prize–winning play (2008) and Oscar-nominated movie (2013) written by Tracy Letts.

Beverly and Violet Weston are the parents of three daughters: Barbara, Ivy, and Karen. In younger years Beverly published a volume of poems that brought him critical acclaim and a bit of fame, but since then his life has been consumed by alcohol and the sense that the life of this world is a big waste. He considers himself "a human cactus." Barbara remembers his saying, "You know, this country was always pretty much a whorehouse, but at least it used to have some promise. Now it's just a shithole."[1] Violet suspects that one of the reasons he has lived such a sad, despondent life was because he couldn't handle the guilt of an old affair with her sister that produced a son. Early in the play Beverly goes missing. He will eventually be found by police at the bottom of a lake, having taken his own life.

Violet has endured a painful life of her own, a life punctuated with bitter disappointments, embarrassments, and too much humiliation at the hands of a mean mother. Married life has been hard too. Beverly once characterized their marriage as a "cruel covenant." It has seen its periods of separation. Violet now suffers from mouth cancer. She feels unappreciated and abandoned by her family, cast aside like a piece of garbage. She hardly eats. She survives by taking a wide assortment of painkillers and anti-anxiety medications. Her medicated state, however, has the side effect of causing her to lash out at those around her. At the lunch after Beverly's funeral, following one of Violet's vicious outbursts, Barbara attempts to take her pills away. Violet exclaims, "Y'see these little blue babies? These are my best fucking friends and they never let me down. Try to get 'em away from me, and I'll eat you alive."[2] A brawl ensues.

As the story unfolds, we gradually learn of the pain each family member carries inside. Each one has a history that is laced with hurts, accidents, and mistakes. Barbara has returned with her husband, Bill, and their fourteen-year-old daughter, Jean. Barbara and Bill have recently separated, because Bill, a college professor, is sleeping with one of his students. Having shared a bed with Bill for twenty-three years, Barbara now finds herself alone and in incredible pain. They can't speak to each other without eventually getting into a fight. She asks him, "Do I bore you, intimidate you, disgust you?" Not long thereafter, she says, "I fail. As a sister, as a mother, as a wife. I fail."[3] Watching him leave for the last time, she sobs that she still loves him. But there is so much hurt, unkindness, and guilt that she can't possibly see what she should do. Watching her family unravel, she says love is a "crock of shit."

The youngest sister, Karen, has arrived with her fiancé, Steve, an entrepreneur, who will eventually be caught trying to have sex with Barbara's daughter, Jean. Karen's life has not at all turned out as she hoped. She has had a parade of disappointing men. She blames herself, even loathes herself, thinking each failed relationship must be her fault. Even after discovering Steve's infidelity, she decides to stick with him. Though horrified and embarrassed, she says, "I'm not defending him. He's not perfect. Just like all the rest of us, down here in the muck. I'm no angel myself. I've done some things I'm not proud of. . . . I may even have to do some things I'm not proud of *again*."[4] When she leaves later with Steve, it is clear that she is terrified to be alone, even if that means a life of betrayal and disappointment.

Ivy, the middle daughter, has been the lone daughter to stay home and keep an eye on mom and dad. She has long felt that her sisters abandoned her and the family. She knows she was not her mother's favorite child. Not having had many boyfriends, she has had to face the teasing of her mom and her mom's sister, Aunt Mattie Fae. But recently she has fallen in love with her cousin Charles. She has kept it a secret for a while, but her announcement that they plan to move to New York City to start a life together prompts Mattie

Fae to reveal to Barbara that Charles is in fact Ivy's half brother, the product of her and Beverly's affair. When Violet and Barbara tell Ivy this to her face, Ivy is devastated. She leaves, promising, "You will never see me again."[5]

The story of the Weston family is the story of the dissolution of love and life. The more we learn of their history, the more we see that they are each terribly wounded and thus incapacitated in multiple ways. They can't receive each other as gifts to be nurtured and celebrated, because their perception is so clouded by loneliness and pain. They can't really live, let alone thrive, because they have been knocked down by life and by each other's resentments, jealousy, and petty plays for position. They have been made insecure and anxious by feelings of guilt, abandonment, and failure, and they have taken the wind out of each other's sails by their slights and neglect. The more their hearts pump, the more they ache. By story's end, each family member has refused love as the movement that turns people *outward* and *toward* each other. Instead, each has slowly turned *inward* and *away* from the other, in a desperate attempt to survive. As the curtain draws to a close, Violet mutters to Johnna, the housekeeper she hardly knows, "And then you're gone, and then you're gone. . . ."

It is tempting to dismiss this story as a farce. So much has gone so wrong! Are families really this screwed up?

Of course, not every family is. But when we take the time to peer behind the Norman Rockwell image of happy family gatherings, it doesn't take very long to discover the loneliness and insecurity that often mark, and in some cases even define, the lives of the people gathered around the table. For any number of reasons, people carry the feeling of being unappreciated, unwanted, or simply slighted in some way. As a result, they find it difficult to move into their own lives with confidence, hope, or joy. Not feeling deeply loved and valued, they also find it difficult to be a nurturing presence to others. They can't make the loving movement outward to embrace and celebrate others, because they are locked within their own pain.

Formed in Sin

BECAUSE SIN IS SUCH a debilitating power, it is hard to imagine that people willingly choose to sin. Why would people decide to live in ways that incapacitate and degrade or that lead to loneliness and hate (even self-hatred)?

Some Christians have argued that sin is something people are born into. It is not a matter of personal choice or decision. Simply by being human, you are in it. Sin is like an infected or messed-up gene that has gotten into the human DNA and screwed it all up from the inside. You don't choose your DNA. You are stuck with it as the inheritance that comes your way whether you like it or not. Rather than you choosing sin, sin chooses you and then holds you tight in its grip.

This teaching often goes by the name "original sin." In its most contested yet consistent formulation it states that a newborn is mired in sin even though the infant has hardly had a thought or made a decision. Based on a reading of the apostle Paul, the story goes like this. God created the world without sin, but owing to the catastrophic decision of Adam to disobey God, all people coming after him are sinners and thus subject to sin's punishment, which is death. "Therefore, just as sin came into the world through one man, and death came through sin, and so death spread to all because all have sinned" (Rom. 5:12). Adam's decision and its consequences cannot be restricted to Adam alone. All people are condemned in Adam's wake, even that newborn infant who has yet to do a wicked thing (which is why Augustine, one of the most influential framers of this position, said that a dead unbaptized infant is consigned to hell). Adam was the first

to have the infected gene, and because he is the forefather of everyone, everyone is a carrier and on their way to punishment.

Why think this way? Doesn't it make a mockery of the human
will and its freedom to choose between good and evil? Other
Christians have certainly thought so and have therefore rejected
the teaching of original sin, arguing that it would be a cruel God
who punishes everyone regardless of the decisions they have made.
Moreover, what would be the point of asking people to obey God
if, against or despite their wills, they were necessarily bound to
disobey because of the inescapable (genetic) inheritance of sin? Pelagius, one of Augustine's most vocal critics, argued that original sin is
a dangerous teaching, because in denying human freedom to choose
good or evil people are, in effect, made to look like robots who
simply act out a predetermined fate. Original sin is really a wicked
teaching, because it degrades human beings by depriving them of
their freedom to choose their future.

It is a curious and paradoxical thing, however, that Pelagius's attempt to champion human freedom and dignity had the unintended
consequence of unleashing profound anxiety. If freedom of choice
is crucial, then *everything* about one's fate depends on the choices
individuals make. It's all up to you! There is no room for screw-
ups and no excuse for the fact that in many instances people "make
choices" in less than ideal circumstances—without sufficient information or understanding, under intense peer pressure, in a compromised mental, physical, or emotional state, and so on. To escape
punishment, however that is conceived, individuals have to become
gold-medal Olympians at goodness. There simply is no excuse for
lackluster performance.

Augustine, on the other hand, could be much more generous in
his counsel to people, saying, in effect: "You are going to screw up,
but that is okay, because God's grace does not depend on your being
perfect. Don't try to set yourself up as the holiest person because,
really, you are no better than anyone else. Everybody sins, so get

over it! Everybody needs God's forgiveness and healing." Besides being democratizing—we are all in the same boat—Augustine's position, despite whatever problems it may have in other areas, has the merit of taking the pressure off people to be perfect.

It is not necessary, however, to hold to something like the genetic or biological transmission of sin to still affirm the unchosen grip that sin can have on people's lives. Think of it not as parents passing on an infected gene to their children, but rather a distorted and corrupt version of love. The story might go something like this. When parents have children, they often have all sorts of aspirations and goals in mind for them. They want them to be successful, liked by others, athletic, beautiful, intelligent, leaders—the list goes on and on. But parents rarely produce the children they want. Why? Because children are their own unique beings. They shouldn't be made to live up to their parent's hopes and expectations or be asked to be something other than who they are. Most every child inevitably falls short because the expectations were set long before the child was born and without a detailed consideration of the child's abilities and desires. Those who try to meet every parental wish discover that they have failed to be themselves.

Why do parents have these expectations? The reasons are legion, ranging from a sense of their own inadequacy to the simple desire to have their children do "better" than they themselves have done. Too often parents hope that their children will compensate for their own failings, or they simply want to be in a position where they can control their children's lives. But from the child's point of view, this predicament is a disaster, because what the child is learning is that love is conditional: parental love is contingent upon whether or not the child achieves the goals that have been set. Love is portrayed and modeled as a quid pro quo reality: *if* you do this, *then* I will give you my love. In a context like this, children cannot feel or experience love as unconditional. They cannot see that they are loved and worthy of being cherished for being the unique people that they are. And so they grow up feeling deficient or defective—a big disappointment.

The love of God is not like this. It is unconditional and universal, extending to every creature and every person. The apostle Paul was clear in saying that even though people sin, Jesus did not hesitate to give himself completely for their salvation (Rom. 5:8). No matter what people do, God will continue to offer himself through Jesus in acts of nurture and care. Why? Because the love of God always wants to be intimate with the beloved, an ever-ready and constant source of encouragement and empowerment. Paul communicated this beautifully when he said that nothing can stop or get in the way of God's desire to love: "For I am convinced that neither death, nor life, nor angels, nor rulers, nor things present, nor things to come, nor powers, nor height, nor depth, nor anything else in all creation, will be able to separate us from the love of God in Christ Jesus our Lord" (Rom. 8:38–39).

When love is presented as a quid pro quo, children can't really love themselves, because who they are is not good enough. Not being able to love themselves, they cannot really love others either. Not having been appreciated for the unique beings that they are, they will likely be unable to affirm and celebrate others in their uniqueness. The relationships they have going forward will likely bear the stamp of a deformed and corrupted love. One of the greatest gifts parents can give their children is the unwavering assurance that they are loved no matter what. Of course, parents and kids will disagree about things. In many instances the disagreement is a good thing, because it helps us see things from another's point of view. The crucial thing, however, is not to let disagreement be the basis for division or the withholding of love.

Although I use this example, my point is not to say that all the problems of this world can be attributed to bad parenting. It is, rather, to show how something as basic as the family unit, one of the places where people learn so much about what it means to be a human being, can shape in decisive ways what people think about love and what skills and sensitivities they will learn moving forward. Multiple other contexts do the same thing: fashion and beauty industries tell people they are worthy *if* they look a certain way; spouses let each other know that the marriage will thrive *if* certain conditions are met; teachers communicate to their students that they are good *if* they make an "A" grade; bosses tell their employees they are valuable only *if* they perform in certain sorts of ways; politicians let citizens know that they matter *if* they think they can get their vote; and preachers tell their parishioners that God loves them *if* they believe this or that or do this or that. The message of love that many people hear, the meaning of love that many people experience, and thus also the ideal that many people are taught to pursue is a conditional love that will be given only when certain conditions are met.

Conditional love is but one form of the corruption of love. Other major forms are pornography, where people's bodies are objectified in the interest of control and profit, and nationalism, where people's affection and gratitude for their country are turned into a cause that is claimed to be beyond questioning or fault. The perennial temptation, it seems, is to restrict or limit love to a sphere in which people can feel safe and exercise control. When this happens, boundaries are drawn and the exercise of love does not extend to people who are unlike those in the "in" class, race, or ideological persuasion.

But genuine love is not like that. What the gospels teach is that God's love extends to everything, every place, and everyone. The circle of love only ever wants to expand until, ultimately, nothing is left outside and alone.

When people are trained to see corrupted love as normal, even as the ideal, they are caught in the grip of sin, because sin is the power at work in the world that prevents people from knowing and participating in the unmerited, undeserved love of God. Sin damages life because it leads to the construction of counterfeit gods and destructive practices that keep people trapped in loneliness, abusive relationships, and desperate or degrading circumstances.

Sin is a powerful force that wounds all the life of this world. It is a corrupting disposition that causes us to walk through this world as if through a cloud of darkness: no one and no thing can be seen in the light of God's love or properly received as a divine gift to be cherished. The power of this corruption goes deep, extending all the way to God, who is now presented as a bully, a merciless judge, or an indifferent sovereign. The great tragedy in Christianity's history is this perverted image of God that then serves to compound and become the justification for sin.

CHAPTER 8

From Intimacy to Idolatry:
The Origins of Sin

If we say that we have no sin, we deceive ourselves,
and the truth is not in us.
1 JOHN 1:8

In your hearts you devise wrongs; your hands deal out violence on earth.
PSALM 58:2

I T WOULD BE A mistake to say that all the pain and suffering of this world is the direct result of distorted love. Sometimes terrible things just happen: a river floods and people lose their homes and the things they love in the high water; two vehicles collide on a foggy, slippery road; a child is stung by a jellyfish while swimming on a coastal beach; people are born with a birth defect or a debilitating disease; or a tsunami destroys multiple villages and kills hundreds of people. The list could go on and on.

But it is also clear that in many instances the suffering people experience does ultimately find an origin in corrupted love. How does corrupted love happen? The task of this chapter is to shed some light on how love becomes distorted and perverted. Sometimes the perversion and suffering are obvious and direct, as when people verbally or physically abuse family members. Other times they are indirect and less obvious, as when people participate in an unjust agricultural system that consigns workers (many of them undocumented migrants) and animals (most of them unseen) to cruel treatment. The people purchasing unjustly produced food are not moral monsters. They do not wake up in the morning plotting how they will oppress the people and creatures that feed them! Even so, their actions and desires, most notably the desire for cheap (and often unhealthy) food, require that many creatures will suffer, including those eating the food produced by this system. They are among the many morally culpable participants in an unjust and anonymous food economy. More on this later.

Love's distortion and corruption work in subterranean, though nonetheless systemic, ways and often have effects that people do not see or intend. If the goal is to minimize the pain and suffering that are attributable to sin, we must understand how sin gets going in the first place. We need to ask: How does a human heart become sick, and what are the patterns of desire and behavior that lead people into degrading and destructive forms of life?

For the beginnings of an answer, we can return to the Garden of Eden, because it is here that we witness an archetypal story of the origins of sin, sickness, and shame. In the story of Adam and Eve we can see how the intimacy of love—the movement that opens and turns people toward each other in postures of welcome, hospitality, and celebration—becomes degraded so that people now turn inward, away, and against each other.

Renouncing Intimacy

WE PICK UP THE garden story with God saying that it is not good for the human to be alone (Gen. 2:18). This is vitally important: *human beings are created for intimacy.* People need to be in relationship, because it is only through life-nurturing relationships that people can fully become themselves. The place of intimacy is the indispensable training ground where people can explore and discern who they are and what makes for the best possible life. This is where they can learn if their self-understanding is honest and their ambition appropriate. Intimacy is the place where a safe, nurturing space is created to explore personal hopes and fears. It is also where we can address a propensity to lie to and violate others. To be in intimate relationship with others means that we can stand before them without shame, because our presence is a life-giving and life-affirming one.

Birds and animals are created by God as potential partners for the first human, but upon meeting them and then naming them (naming being an important way of stating the identity of and way to relate to another), Adam realizes they are not suitable. Though important to human life in multiple ways, animals are not the sorts of creatures with which humans can be fully intimate. So while the man is asleep, God takes a rib from him and forms it into the first woman, a fellow person, and one who shares the same kind of being and possibility. The promise of intimacy now has its first chance at fulfillment.

It is important to note that sameness of being does not mean sameness of life, nor does intimacy with another mean the smothering or eclipse of the one by the other. In this story humanity is differentiated into a man and a woman. The *difference,* however, is not a *division* or *divide,* because each person shares intimately in the flesh and bone of the other. Difference is a good thing, because with the appearance of someone genuinely other, the prospect of a world beyond oneself emerges. To meet another who is not the same as me means that I can learn from the other, appreciate the other's point of view, and potentially be of service to the other as we explore life together. We can "share bread" (the root meaning of a "companion") and taste the rich diversity of life's flavors. People need each other, but they also need to learn to respect the integrity of others and appreciate the things that make them unique, because it is mutuality worked out in a context of difference that opens the fullness of life's possibilities.

Upon seeing her, the man is clearly thrilled at the prospect of the intimacy that is now possible: "This at last is bone of my bones and flesh of my flesh" (Gen. 2:23). By joining together, they now have the opportunity to become "one flesh" and share in a life of mutual belonging and exploration. They can come together in marital union and fidelity and in their love for each other discover the life of paradise.

Scripture says, "And the man and his wife were both naked, and were not ashamed" (2:25). Why did the writer of this story include the detail about their being naked? To be naked before another is to be completely vulnerable and to be seen for who one is (wrinkles and blemishes and all!). It's just you, with no other distractions, with nothing to hide, and with nothing to give except yourself. To be naked is to be without an agenda and to desire to give yourself wholly or completely to another, so that in your life together you can become "one flesh." What is possible now is the kind of intimacy that makes mutual nurture and celebration come alive. To stand naked and freely before others is to stand before them without shame or guilt. In this moment there is no pornographic desire or objectification of the other, only the willingness to give and receive. As we will see, it is with the appearance of shame that people first feel the need to turn *away* from each other, because exploitation has infected the relationship.

At this stage in the story the man and the woman share a life that is right, healthy, and whole because they "know" each other—

through the intimacy of embodied touching—to be committed to the care of each other. They have not used their freedom for their own advantage, but have instead focused it on the flourishing of the other. They are married to each other, which means they have pledged their hearts and their skill and energy to each other. Out of their fidelity and love, new life—in the forms of children, a welcoming home, but also a fruitful garden world—can arise. Marital love is a training ground for the exercise of care in the world. It is where people learn the attention, commitment, and mercy they need to nurture each other even when they screw up. If spouses cannot learn to love each other in ways that liberate each other into the fullness of life, it is unlikely that they will be able to do the same for their children or for others more generally.

Another way to put this is to say that marital love is another form of the hospitality God manifests in the creating of the world as a whole. As Genesis presents it and as we have already seen, God's gardening and hospitable ways with the world create the conditions for delight. The delight described here follows from the intimate involvement of a gardener who, devoted to the garden, is *close* enough to see life unfold in its various, sometimes difficult stages, *committed* enough to assist when assistance is needed, *humble* enough not to try to impose a design or plan where it is not welcome, and *gracious* enough to stand back and help another become what the other is meant to become. Successful gardeners work to create the conditions in which plants can flourish. In like manner, spouses work to create the conditions in which their beloved can thrive.

God creates people, so that they too can practice the intimacy that leads to mutual delight. But for that possibility to be realized, people must learn the arts of hospitality and care. The first human is put in the garden and told to take care of it, an instruction that is not presented as a curse (Gen. 2:15). It is, rather, the regular and practical way in which human beings can directly experience the freshness and vitality, but also the need and fragility, of life. To appreciate life's fullness and abundance, it is essential that people get close enough to know each other (it is significant that one sense of the Hebrew term for "knowing" entails the intimacy of sexual union, e.g., Gen. 4:1). To know another you have to be *with* the other; and to genuinely be with the other, you need to figure out how to stay helpful even when one or both of you are difficult, in pain, or simply unwelcoming. Creatures *need* each other, live *from* each other, *through* each other, and *to* each other. The truth of this position is confirmed every time a creature eats, drinks, breathes, or procreates. To "be" is to "be together." To thrive is to thrive together. *There is no real life apart from life together.*

As the story progresses, we discover that the practice of intimacy is not easy. It is hard to give yourself to another in nonviolating ways and in modes that nurture the unique potential of the other's life. You are tempted to want to have others serve you, or at least do the things that you want. Put another way, the heart becomes sick and desire distorted the moment people want to have life on their own terms, the moment they think they are above question or beyond fault. Sin is a kind of dishonesty in which people deny their dependence on and need of each other. To see how this happens, we need to appreciate the significance of one of the trees in the garden.

Freedom and Restraint

GOD TOLD THE MAN, "You may eat freely of every tree of the garden; but of the tree of the knowledge of good and evil you shall not eat, for in the day that you eat of it you shall die" (Gen. 2:16–17). Why is this one tree forbidden? Many answers have been offered over the years. One says that the knowledge of good and evil represents the establishment of boundaries or limits: some actions are permissible or beneficial, and some are not. This means that for life to go well, people cannot simply do as they please. Being a human creature means you can't have it all. People need to know that there are limits that must be observed because without limits we will forget that we are beings that *need* and *depend* on others. Which is why they must learn to practice restraint.

Restraint is crucial. When I know that it is wrong for me to act in certain ways, I simultaneously affirm the integrity of others by acknowledging that my behavior can potentially violate them. To practice restraint, I must be able to stand back and see that the exercise of my freedom can become disordered and injurious. There are limits to what I can and cannot do: this is what honest intimacy teaches. Limits protect the integrity of others. When I acknowledge the sanctity and value of another, I am better able to see why I should be grateful for and a source of help to another. A well-ordered life, one that results in healthy relationships, is one that presupposes the double capacity to get out of the way of another, so as not to impede flourishing, and to be available to help, so that together both can sort out what true flourishing actually looks like. It is not easy to hold both of these capacities in balance.

To eat from the tree of the knowledge of good and evil amounted to the consumption and thus the erasure of all limits. In this act the need for restraint vanished. When Adam and Eve ate the fruit, they indicated that they wanted to be little gods beholden to no one, able to exercise personal freedom however they wanted. What they did not realize is that a life without limits amounts to a life of degradation and dissolution. Why does unrestrained freedom lead to the wounding of life? Because when one lives without restraint, one acts in ways that inevitably violate the integrity of others. To deny the sanctity of creatures, a sanctity that is grounded in God's love for them, is to put oneself in a position to exploit them.

It is with the appearance of *exploitation* that the need to turn away from others finds its first expression. *The origins of sin and shame*

are to be found in the distorted desire that refuses intimacy and instead seeks
power, control, or simply convenience.

What Adam and Eve failed to appreciate is that the power they
sought does not at all reflect the love of God. God does not violate
creatures. Instead, God welcomes, nurtures, and liberates creatures
to be themselves. God's hospitable, gardening way with the world is
the very opposite of the carefree, care-less life they think they will
obtain by eating from this tree. But it is too late. Having succumbed
to the temptation, the man and the woman see for the first time
that they need to be ashamed of themselves. "Then the eyes of both
were opened, and they knew that they were naked; and they sewed
fig leaves together and made loincloths for themselves" (Gen. 3:7).
Upon denying the need for restraint and thereby also denying the
integrity and sanctity of others, they want to hide. Being ashamed,
they can no longer be naked.

The appearance of shame in the garden represents a profound
degradation of love and is a sure sign that the heart has become sick.
Shame signifies a broken and disordered relationship. It indicates
that one's own freedom has become dishonest and violent, because
it violates the freedom of another creature. The garden, rather than
being the place in which creatures are welcomed, nurtured, and enjoyed, now becomes a scene of competitive striving in which people
feel no need to restrain themselves or respect others. They can take
and consume at will. It is but a short step from this carefree, loveless
disposition to the murder that Cain commits against his brother,
Abel. Cain did not appreciate his brother as a creature deserving respect and care (after the murder he responds to God by asking, "Am
I my brother's keeper?" [4:9], thereby showing his negligent frame
of mind). He saw him as a challenge and threat to his own freedom.
Given the absence of restraint and the failure to love, it made perfect
sense for him to eliminate the challenge.

And so a garden scene that began with the man and the woman

naked before each other, prepared to become one flesh of mutual nurture and delight, has now ended in murder. Rather than standing without shame, fully facing and open to each other, humans now feel the need to look away and hide. They are ashamed because they have used their freedom to turn against each other.

The power and depth of this story are easily missed if we think that Adam and Eve were malicious or demonic brutes. They weren't. We understand them better—and thus also our own condition—if we can learn to appreciate the anxiety that saturated their wayward movements. To see what I mean, consider that Adam and Eve had to face the most fundamental of questions: How will we respond to the gift of life, both our own and that of others?

It is easy to say that life is a gift. It is another matter to understand that the acknowledgment of life as a gift entails living in the world in particular sorts of ways. More specifically, it means that we need to reposition ourselves as persons who do not *possess* and *control* life, but continually *receive* and *share* it. If life is a gift that means it is not our invention. It is not something we can do with as we please. As a gift, life comes with its own integrity, carrying what is sometimes called its sacred and miraculous character. To see that life is a miracle and then receive it as such, we need to figure out what life is ultimately for *on its terms* and then order our desires appropriately. We need, most basically, to get our fear and ambition out of the way, so that what we receive is genuinely a gift and not an extension or fulfillment of the desires we happen to have. The temptation is to want to have life on our terms, because then we can be in control and keep ourselves comfortable and secure.

Life comes from beyond our comprehension, even beyond our imagination, which is why it should be an occasion for perpetual amazement, humility, and gratitude. Author Annie Dillard puts it wisely when she says:

It could be that our faithlessness is a cowering cowardice
born of our very smallness, a massive failure of imagination.
Certainly nature seems to exult in abounding radicality,
extremism, anarchy. If we were to judge nature by its common
sense or likelihood, we wouldn't believe the world existed. In
nature, improbabilities are the one stock in trade. The whole
creation is one lunatic fringe. If creation had been left up to
me, I'm sure I wouldn't have had the imagination or courage
to do more than shape a single, reasonably sized atom, smooth
as a snowball, and let it go at that. No claims of any and all
revelations could be so far-fetched as a single giraffe.[1]

Dillard describes our difficulty as a failure of faith and courage, because it takes tremendous discipline and affection to affirm, let alone nurture, a life that is of no pragmatic use to us or that may even be a challenge to the kind of life we would like to enjoy. It is much easier, much more comforting, to take and remake the given world into a place that is geared to our control and satisfaction, which is why we do not approach others naked but instead armed with spreadsheets, business models, heavy machinery, or weapons. The acknowledgment that life is a gift means that it is not exclusively for us and for our gratification. It does not exist on our terms.

So many of the histories of human settlement and economic development communicate that we do not want to *receive* the world. We'd much rather *take* it. Transactions are not conducted in the language of amazement and awe or humility and gratitude. Being pragmatists, we approach the world through a lens that reduces things and people to "units" of production and profitability. Though we are sometimes shocked by the presence of slavery in our histories, the logic of loveless thinking and acting must finally lead us there. When love is distorted, the sanctity of others is denied, and the way is made for us to turn each other into commodities and property that exist to serve the ends the powerful choose.

The primary recognition that we are creatures who need each other—for help and companionship, for food and inspiration, for care and celebration—can be overwhelming. Do we want to go very deep into an exploration and then admission of our own need? Do we want to acknowledge that our own well-being depends on what others must do for us? Sometimes the immensity of our need weighs so heavily upon us that we would rather deny it and present a façade of self-sufficiency. We are then tempted to believe that we can live on our own, out of our own ability and resources. Our bodies, however, show that this strategy is a lie. We have to eat. We yearn for the touch of another. We each depend on the hands of help and the words of encouragement that others provide. And so *we become anxious in the face of our own need.*

When faced with our own need, it is tempting to turn away from others, believing that we have nothing to give. But in withholding what we are uniquely suited to give—and every creature has something to give to others—we abandon the world. It is also tempting to give into the fear that what we give might be rejected and so not even make the attempt to help. To give to another is to share oneself with another. What we give is not just the thing given, but also the love that is embodied in the gift. It can be excruciating to find one's love, the very core of oneself, rejected. What does such rejection say about me? Does it mean that I am unworthy of being loved by another? The occasions for anxiety are endless.

The story of Adam and Eve reveals the profound implications that follow from refusing to receive the world as a gift. Though they were presented a world in which everything they needed was provided, Adam and Eve could not receive it gratefully and nurture it carefully. Their grasping and taking of life—their eating of the forbidden fruit—bear witness to the exploitation and destruction that follow from the anxiety that arises in the face of shared need and responsibility. In wanting to take life on their own terms, they also refused to see others as God's love made material. In this refusal they lost the ability to cherish each other. They lost the intimacy that makes for an abundant life.

The inability, even the refusal, to reside faithfully and shamelessly in the spaces of intimacy is a sure sign that love has become distorted and corrupt. In this corruption we can begin to appreciate how a heart becomes sick and sinful.

From Anxiety to Idolatry

ANOTHER WAY TO UNDERSTAND the corruption of love is to examine how an idolatrous impulse comes to reside within human hearts. As a fundamental distortion of love, idolatry transforms intimacy in which *others are cherished, served, and empowered,* into forms of bondage in which *others are made to serve us.* To be idolatrous is to be incapable of delighting in things as they are, because they are now seen as valuable only insofar as they serve personal needs, desires, and expectations.

As commonly presented, idolatry is the worship of a false god. The problem, according to this presentation, is that we are sometimes mistaken about who the true god is. The solution is to identify the right god, and then everything will be fine.

This account overlooks idolatry's fundamental character. People become idolatrous because they can't get past worshipping themselves. The primary problem is confused worship.

Genuine worship is meant to take us beyond ourselves to the source of life, which we clearly did not create. What we find in idolatry, however, is a gesture that keeps us at the center of everything, realigning each creature so that its value is determined by us. It is important to recall that idols are things that people make or establish, which means that an idol is by definition the object that we think will erase our fears and fulfill our desires. When we make an idol out of anything, we at the same time make that thing serve the interests we bring to it. We make idols because we believe the things we worship will save us.

Consider the classic biblical story of idolatry. The Israelites, freshly freed from their time as slaves in Egypt, are wandering through the wilderness, a place that by definition is unfamiliar and not under their control. They are afraid and anxious, hungry and thirsty. They are unsure about their future and wonder if they will ever enjoy a good and happy life. They do not trust their leader Moses, who tells them to put their trust in God, and so they decide to take matters into their own hands.

While Moses is on Mount Sinai, the people gather around Aaron, Moses's right-hand man. They have become impatient and say, "Come, make gods for us, who shall go before us; as for this Moses, the man who brought us up out of the land of Egypt, we do not know what has become of him" (Exod. 32:1). But what kind of god could this possibly be if it exists only as a response to their impatience and insecurity? Aaron instructs them to bring whatever gold they are wearing. He forms the gold into the shape of a calf, saying, "These are your gods, O Israel, who brought you up out of the land of Egypt!" (32:4). A single calf, yet multiple gods? A sign, perhaps, that the calf represents the many different anxieties of the people contributing the gold.

Aaron then builds an altar before the calf and announces a festival for the next day, a festival at which people bring their offerings and sacrifices of well-being. By making offerings to the calf the people demonstrate that they now put their hope and trust in it. Their worship of the calf, however, is really a worship of themselves, because the calf only exists as the material reflection of the anxiety and desire that prompted them to create it in the first place. Their trust and hope is not in the calf. It is really in themselves. Having put themselves in charge, the people eat and drink and revel at the proceedings.

Moses returns from the mountain and is hot with anger. He sees in the golden calf a rejection of God and the arrogant assertion of a people. He burns the calf, grinds what is left into powder, scatters it on the water, and then makes the people drink it (a fitting conclusion, since the calf that came out of them is now being returned to them). He then asks Aaron how this wicked act of idolatry came to be. Wanting to be absolved of responsibility, Aaron replies that the people begged him to make the calf. He merely collected the gold, threw it into a fire, and "out came this calf" (apparently of its own doing!). Meanwhile, the people are out of control, wildly running about, suggesting that chaos is the logical end of competing idolatries.

To make an idol of anything is to place upon it an expectation it cannot bear. When we mistake a creature for the Creator, we then expect that creature to give, sustain, and fulfill life. No creature can do this, because creatures by definition are finite and contingent beings who depend on others for their own lives. Moreover, when we expect a creature to calm our fears or satisfy our ambitions, we invariably make that creature serve an end that is alien to its own fulfillment. The creature is thereby violated and wounded. A primary reason for why idolatry is such an affront to God is because it harms the creatures God loves. Idolatry and intimacy are mutually exclusive.

The crucial element in idolatry is the installation of anything as a savior or solution to our problems. Idols evoke worship in us, because we think they can save us from life's contingencies, mysteries, and finitude. Put another way, we make idols of all sorts of things—the stock market, a job or company, our family—because we think that by giving our allegiance to them our lives will be made secure and complete. Viewed pragmatically, stock markets can increase our monetary wealth, jobs can give meaning and shape to our daily schedules, and families can provide us with a sense of belonging and support. But none of these things in and of themselves have the power to give us or hold us within life. Stock markets crash, jobs are outsourced, and family members eventually disappoint or depart.

This does not make them evil. Received properly, they are each gifts given by God to enhance life. But when we pin unrealistic hopes on them, forgetting that it is God alone who provides and sustains us all, we turn a gift into an idol. We are mistaken about where the power of life and life's true fulfillment ultimately reside. We also violate the integrity of others by making them serve personal insecurities and idolatrous fantasies. Ultimately, our confusion leads to the degradation of whatever we make into an idol. God's commandment against idolatry is God's way of saying, "Receive creation as a gift from me. Do not make the gift something it is not—a private possession, the object of your fancy, or the hope of your salvation—for when you do, you will harm or destroy it and bring harm to yourselves."

Idolatry is a confused gesture that unleashes destruction upon the world. Why? Because idolatry is a distortion of love. Rather than making room for other creatures to become themselves, idolatry makes creatures serve us. Hospitality is thereby twisted into a situation whereby the world is held hostage. In every idolatrous move, creatures are made to serve the fear, insecurity, and ambition we feel. Creatures can no longer be themselves. They must be made to serve whatever desires we have. Idolatry is the imposition of the self upon the world for the purpose of the self's comfort, control, and glorification. In this imposition we find the most basic and systemic form of the world's degradation.

Idolatry affects everyone. It is like the default setting by which people tend to operate. You don't need to be a moral monster to reduce others to the scale of your concerns. All you need to be is afraid, insecure, or impatient. All you need to do is replace a primary trust in God with an exclusive trust in yourself.

We should not be surprised that idolatry has led us to so much of the world's destruction. When the meaning and significance and thus also the goodness and beauty of things are reduced to what we want, then the only limit to action is our appetite and desire. Given that our desires differ, it is all but inevitable that our idolatries will clash and result in soils degraded, waters exhausted, air polluted, mountains detonated, plants poisoned, species exterminated, forests felled, animals abused, workers exploited, people made sick, and communities wasted. So much of the destruction of the world is the effect of its reduction to the scope of our fears and anxieties.

The logic of idolatry is ultimately self- and world-defeating, because the idolatrous impulse is born out of a deep distrust in God's love and care and a denial of the sacred character of the world. People embark on an idolatrous path when they believe that God's gifts are not sufficient or God's care is misdirected. They begin to think that they must take hold of the world for themselves. But to do so they must first unmoor others from their life in God, so that they can now find their life in us. In this unmooring and remooring, humanity takes the place of God, hospitality is transformed into hostility, and the world becomes a place of wounds.

Eating Our Way out of Intimacy

IDOLATRY IS ORDINARY. WE don't need to make golden calves or other graven images to participate in it. To see how the logic of idolatry and thus also the deformation of love takes root in the most mundane of activities, we can consider the way we eat.

We should not be surprised that eating the fruit of the tree of the knowledge of good and evil precipitated the wounding of life, because eating is humanity's most profound and intimate engagement with the processes of life. Our ways of eating—what we eat, how we eat it, and with whom—are the daily demonstration of whether we are capable of receiving life as a gift. Every time we enter a kitchen or sit down at a table to dine, we communicate that we are one member within a vast membership of creatures that are nurture and food for each other. Every time we take a bite, we signal that we need soil and water, worms and bees, and the many processes of decomposition and growth that keep eating on the move. Every time we swallow, we take into our bodies the life and death of another creature. We don't simply live *alongside* others. At the gustatory level, others come *inside*. What could be more intimate than that? Eating is the daily activity that joins us to others in bonds of necessity and nutrition that regularly exceed our deserving or comprehension.

Eating is no trifling activity. For any creature to eat, other creatures must die, most often by being eaten themselves. The soil that is the basis for the fertility, growth, and enjoyment of all terrestrial life is also one vast feeding frenzy in which billions of organisms live and die together. Life as we know it depends on death. That means death is not simply the end of life; it is life's steadfast companion. There is no sharing in life that is not also a sharing in another's death. Acknowledging this is terrifying. How does any one of us become worthy of another's death and communicate that its life is not trivial or to be engaged recklessly? One more reason to be anxious!

Much of today's food industry bears the marks of a system that hides and denies the costly grace of food. Rather than acknowledge that food is a holy life-and-death mystery that joins us to each other, today's food providers regularly communicate that eating is reducible to the consumption of commodities. What matters most is that the food purchased is cheap, convenient, and available in abundant supply. The thousands of food products on display in grocery stores and the sheer number of calories being produced show that the industrial methods at work in agriculture and food processing have delivered. Many of today's eaters are spending less of their income on food than ever before. They are spending less time growing and cooking food. They are living a life of "food ease," a life in which they simply walk into a grocery store and naively pluck the commodities that are most appealing to them. In this world the life and death struggles of the garden have been replaced with the thousands of slickly packaged products that communicate it is all about and all for us.

But what could be more ignorant than to eat with the ease of a credit-card swipe? If eating is the daily activity that most intimately joins us to the life and death of the world's creatures, what does the blindness and the anonymity (how many of us really know where our food is coming from?) that saturate today's industrial food economies say about our reception of life?

For people to eat cheaply and conveniently, the world's creatures must be systematically abused. The abuse happens on multiple levels: soil is degraded by the steady application of synthetic fertilizers and ever more toxic herbicides; water is polluted by many chemical and agricultural inputs; vast fields that would otherwise support multiple diverse species of plants, insects, birds, and animals are reduced to monocultures of wheat, corn, soybeans, and cotton; animals are taken off their range and raised in confinement conditions that often breed sickness and unrelenting misery; agricultural workers, many of them undocumented, do backbreaking work for minimal pay and without adequate protection; poor people and racial minorities find themselves in food deserts and swamps, where only food of the lowest nutritional quality is available; and the eaters of all this industrial food find themselves in bodies that are increasingly sickly and overweight owing to the processing of commodities laced with fats and sweeteners. Food, which is supposed to be the sharing and the fellowship of life—the material medium of God's love made nutritious and delectable—has become a pervasive symbol of life's wounding and degradation. With every industrial bite, it seems, we take in a mouthful of shame.

Humans were placed by God in the garden not to naively or selfishly pluck and consume its fruit. They were put there to work and take care of the garden's life, because it is through daily attention and nurture that people learn to appreciate the potential and the vulnerability, but also the integrity and grace, of creatures. They were invited to participate in God's gardening ways with the world, ways that are directed by and experienced as love, because when we care for each other we can stand before each other without shame. But Adam and Eve wanted food on their own terms. As a result they were banished from the garden. They did not really need to be banished by God. They banished themselves. Their loveless way of being, their disposition to take rather than gratefully receive, meant that no creature could possibly be an occasion for delight. Delight in God's good and beautiful gifts was replaced with the desire to have the world on their own terms. Following in their wake, we have become the dispensers of shame.

The origin of sin is to be found in this distorted appetite, in the desires for convenience and comfort, and in ignorance. If we want to know where much of the world's pain and suffering comes from, we can look here.

CHAPTER 9

The Wide Reach of Sin

There is no faithfulness or loyalty, and no knowledge of God in the
land. . . . Therefore the land mourns, and all who live in it languish.
HOSEA 4:1–3

IN THIS CHAPTER WE will see that the reach and the effects of sin
have never been confined to the human realm. Because sin is the
power that distorts love, and because love is the motivation and the
medium of human action, we should not be surprised to learn that
almost all relationships—the ones we have with other people, but
also the relationships we have with places, neighborhoods, and non-
human creatures—will eventually be twisted and mangled because
of sin. Such is the power of sin that even when people are not present, the effects of corrupted love continue to be at work, inflicting
damage in unanticipated ways. Just as love surprises us by inspiring

and accomplishing all sorts of unexpected goodness in the world, so too sin startles us by unleashing multiple forms of unplanned suffering.

One way to think about this is as chain reactions. An act of kindness has the effect of liberating someone else's spirit to act gently and generously, which in turn has the effect of transforming an institution, so that now its members are challenged to live in a more hospitable manner. Without planning it, a small seed of kindness has grown in all sorts of ways, producing flowers and gardens we could not have imagined. Of course, once the flower blooms, few people stop to think about the seed, even though it is clear that the forgotten, unseen seed set the entire process in motion. Who would have thought that a tiny seed holds so much potential?

The beauty of love is that it grows rather than diminishes by giving. Once people become inspired by love, it is impossible to predict or limit the forms of good that can emerge.

In a similar manner, small acts of ill will or neglect multiply in their effect, because the persons injured or slighted now act out of their pain and desperation. An ethos of harm comes to dominate communities and places, through which those who reside there learn to make sense of their lives. They plan their lives according to the injury they expect and become willing participants in economies that extend malevolence in the world. Small acts of ill will, rather than producing a beautiful garden, multiply and spread throughout the workings of communities and cultures, turning them into forces that produce injury and hurt.

The ugliness of sin is such that it infiltrates and wounds everything it touches. Its effects cannot be easily contained. Once sin becomes active, it takes us to places we do not want to go and into a future we would never choose. To see what I mean, we can turn to the coal-mining region of Appalachia.

The Disaster of Sin

SHORTLY AFTER MIDNIGHT ON October 11, 2000, the bottom of a coal-sludge containment pond ruptured, sending 300 million gallons of toxic slurry through an underground mineshaft and into the headwaters of Wolf and Coldwater Creeks. The residents of Inez in Martin County, Kentucky, did not know anything was wrong until several hours later when they saw the sludge streaming down their valley, a massive black lavalike wave inundating everything in its path. Though it was the largest North American environmental disaster east of the Mississippi—a spill nearly thirty times larger than the 1989 *Exxon-Valdez* disaster in Alaska's Prince William Sound—few in the nation would hear about it. On November 29, roughly six weeks after the spill, the Martin County Coal Company released a statement in court: "[The sludge spill] was the direct, sole, and proximate result of an act of God, the occurrence of which was not within the control of Martin County Coal."

Coal sludge, a mixture of water, rock, and clay, contains heavy metals (cadmium, nickel, mercury, and arsenic) and acrylamide, a known carcinogen and lethal neurotoxin. It is created as a byproduct from the washing of coal being prepared for market. Hundreds of containment ponds holding sludge are located throughout Appalachia, some near homes, one immediately above an elementary school. Coal companies rarely build these ponds to safety specifications, nor are they routinely or rigorously inspected by government officials (it was later found that the wall between the pond and the mineshaft was less than 18 feet rather than the claimed 150). Almost none of the permitted ponds have in place the emergency plans required by law.

In 1994, just six years earlier, the same Martin County containment pond released 100 million gallons of sludge. Though multiple recommendations were made at that time to make the pond usable again, and though relatively inexpensive technology existed on-site to filter the water from the sludge, leaving a solid that could then be buried, Martin County Coal Company ignored them all and began filling up the pond on the very same day. Officials of the Mine Safety and Health Administration (MSHA) went on record then saying they had little confidence that another rupture would not occur: "There's nothing here that will prevent a[nother] breakthrough."[1]

An investigation into the 2000 spill began promptly but, as so often happens in coal country, went nowhere. Though the devastation was immense—Martin County resident Mickey McCoy said, "It was like someone poured a huge black milkshake out over the mountain. It just ruined everything"[2]—cleanup efforts were a joke. Slurry is still easily found the moment one moves a clod of earth. Soil that was once fertile now barely sustains a few weeds and sickly trees. Meanwhile, Massey Energy, the parent company of Martin County Coal and a major financial contributor to political leaders, was able to walk away by paying a paltry fine of $5,500.

In coal country, coal companies have little reason to fear the law. Elected and law-enforcement officials are often beholden to coal companies for political and financial support. The government agencies in charge of inspecting mining operations and enforcing the rules often look the other way. As McCoy sees it, "The watchdogs of the environment have become the guard dogs of the coal industry." At one of the local hearings following the spill, Environmental Protection Agency (EPA) officials were visibly chummy with coal-industry lawyers. Noticing that each panelist on the platform was drinking bottled water, Martin County residents said, "Go over there to the damn water fountain. Try the shit we have to drink."[3] Not one of them did. It doesn't take long to come to the conclusion that these people are living in a Kafkaesque world in which the search for justice is futile, perhaps even ridiculous. In this world little is sacred except, of course, the grail of ever increasing profits.

The two spills in Martin County were not unprecedented. Nor were they a surprise. Disaster, disease, and death saturate coal-country history. They are what people have come to expect. Injury has become the widely accepted cost of doing business. Roughly thirty years earlier, on February 26, 1972, in Logan County, West Virginia, a poorly constructed slurry-containment dam collapsed, sending 132 million gallons of water and 1 million tons of coal waste through sixteen coal-mining communities along Buffalo Creek. The communities were demolished. One hundred and twenty-five people were killed; four thousand were left homeless. Whole houses with people inside them could be seen floating to their doom in the flood. People involved in rescue efforts pulled small bodies from the black mud praying that they were dogs rather than babies. Mrs. Withero was buried in mud up to her neck, but survived. Mr. Johnson was found alive in some rubble, completely naked, genitals torn off his body. Ronnie Smith, an area resident, upon seeing fourteen houses destroyed as they hit a bridge, said, "There were many lives lost. It is the most tragic thing I've seen in my life. I'm sorry God let me live to see it."

In his testament to the region, Kentucky lawyer, legislator, and conservationist Harry Caudill wrote:

> Coal has always cursed the land in which it lies. When men begin to wrest it from the earth it leaves a legacy of foul streams, hideous slag heaps and polluted air. It peoples this transformed land with blind and crippled men and with widows and orphans. It is an extractive industry which takes all away and restores nothing. It mars but never beautifies. It corrupts but never purifies.[4]

We can see in the histories of the coal fields of Appalachia how a failure of love produces so much pain and hurt. Here we witness how corporate profits have become the contemporary idol before which everything—children, homes, communities, watersheds, farm fields, mountains, even a viable future—is sacrificed. In the worship of money, all are implicated. Though it is tempting to point the finger at mining executives, even cast them as villains, the truth is that consumers want cheap electricity. Cheap electricity, like cheap food, requires and produces brutality. People living far away from the damage don't want to know about it. We don't want intimacy. We don't want to be reminded of the fact that when we flip the power switch, we should be ashamed about the ruined mountains, the degraded watersheds, the impoverished coal communities, and the diminished futures of young people.

For the most part, consumers of electricity are not malicious. They are not trying to hurt others or damage the world. But they have limited the scope of their love to the rather narrow register of their own comfort, convenience, and want. They have forgotten that the love of God extends to *every* creature and *every* person. Sin produces in people habits of inattention and negligence, so that they can move through a wounded world oblivious to their responsibility for it. It produces forms of blindness and tactics of evasion that leave whole regions and communities of people in a degraded and despairing state.

Acts of God?

It is not uncommon to find coal-company operators blaming God for the misery that they produce. For example, an official speaking on behalf of the owners of the Logan County dam stated: "We're investigating the damage which was caused by the flood, which we believe, of course, was an act of God." All claims of responsibility for the dam's collapse were denied by the Pittston Coal Company.

God had sent down too much rain, and the dam was "simply incapable of holding the water God poured into it."

Coal-company officials are hardly unique in claiming that disasters of this sort are "acts of God." Insurance companies and regulatory bodies regularly chime in with a similar refrain. These claims, however, are plainly self-serving, because they have the effect of absolving officials and companies from any responsibility for the pain and damage caused by a disaster. They are also cruel, because those who could or should have worked to prevent the misery and destruction from happening now want to claim the status of fellow victims. To say that a pond rupture is "the direct, sole, and proximate result of an act of God" means that human arrogance, ignorance, or negligence had no part to play in the events that transpired.

What makes an event an "act of God"? Are tornadoes, earthquakes, hurricanes, floods, and droughts divine acts? In a certain sense they clearly are. As the Creator of the world, God is the power at work within it, nurturing creatures into life. But God does not dictate events, because God's love is not coercive. God, as I argued in Chapter 4, is not a puppeteer manipulating creatures and events—that would make God a Superbeing, the biggest or strongest creature on the block, controlling the many objects of the universe. God is nonetheless mysteriously present as the empowering love that creates a space for creatures to be and to develop. Divine love is hospitable, making room for creatures to exercise their freedom as they attempt to realize their God-given potential. That means creation is a place of spontaneity but also vulnerability, because the freedoms of creatures have the potential to clash or result in abuse.

It is not easy to know how to live harmoniously within this complex and diverse, but ultimately hospitable environment. We don't often know how to exercise our freedoms responsibly or faithfully and thus in ways that promote life. Innumerable creatures and processes must interweave together for flourishing to occur, which means that we need to respect and honor the integrity of others while we attempt to work out our own lives. How shall we weave our lives closely with others without bruising or harming them?

Sometimes we don't understand how God's hospitality works, or we fail to appreciate that the work of divine hospitality includes dimensions of which we are unaware. When an earthquake occurs, for instance, and we witness the devastation to homes and the lives lost, we are tempted to conclude that this event is all bad, perhaps even evil. But is it, especially when we recognize that the movement of tectonic plates is vital to the earth's geological development? Without geological uplift we would not have mountain ranges and all the geographical and ecological diversity they make possible. The floods and tornadoes and droughts that can be so destructive to us are also moments within meteorological processes that are indispensable to life's growth and development.

Saying this is not to explain away evil. Much of it we simply cannot understand, given our limited point of view, which is to say that some forms of evil will remain a mystery calling for a compassionate rather than a comprehending response. In cases like this it is clear that perception and interpretation are primary issues. The temptation is to perceive and thus narrate events according to the narrow register of what we want or don't want to happen. An earthquake destroyed my home. It can't be my fault, though I perhaps should have built it somewhere else or built it in ways that are more structurally sound. Therefore, it must be an act of God.

Some of the events that we narrowly term "acts of God," however, upon closer inspection tell another tale. Is it an act of God when torrential rain and a mountain mudslide destroy a village after the tree and vegetation cover on the hillside—cover that retains water and prevents mudslides—had been removed to make way for inappropriate agriculture? Is it an act of God that people are suffering from multiple diseases when we in the past century have invented thousands of poisons and then systematically applied, through military and agricultural use, millions of gallons of them to our water and soil? Is it an act of God when the rate of extreme weather events increases owing to an atmosphere that has become warmer because of the burning of fossil fuels?

One of humanity's most important tasks is to learn to live within processes and among creatures in ways that show humility, respect, and responsibility. This is not easy. It takes time, the accumulated insight of communities and traditions, and detailed attention to *know where we are* and then live charitably there. Having an idolatrous heart, we so much want the world to suit our own rather than God's purposes. Sometimes we want God to be a controlling puppeteer who manipulates the world into a place of our own liking, if for no other reason than because such a God takes the pressure off us and lessens our responsibility for learning how to live carefully and wisely wherever we are. Acknowledging freedom and thus also responsibility can be a great burden.

The world does not exist for our exclusive satisfaction. It consists of billions of creatures all trying to make their way through life, and God loves them all, even the creatures that can harm us (for more on this point, see Job 38–41). That makes our world a dangerous as well as a delightful place. Oftentimes we don't know enough about what our responsibilities are, which is why we need to move with much greater humility and caution than we often do. It takes a considerable amount of attention, learning, and dedication to live in ways that contribute to God's hospitable ways with the world. It takes vigilance to know where we are and then discipline and good work to live there in ways that contribute to mutual flourishing. Droughts will happen, but it is not inevitable that mass starvation should follow them. Torrential rains will come, but it does not necessarily follow that whole mountain communities will be demolished.

The record shows that mining and regulatory officials in Kentucky and West Virginia were negligent. They knew what needed to be done, *but looked away*. Negligence represents the exact opposite of God's attentive, hospitable ways with creation. To be negligent is to refuse fidelity to a people and their place and is therefore also an abandonment of love. Massey Energy and the Pittston Coal Company sought their own benefit—which is to say, they sought the benefit of their shareholders, people like you and me who have our retirement funds invested in their practices—rather than the well-being of creatures and communities. Buffalo Creek resident Shirley Marcum understood this: "I didn't see God a-driving them slate trucks up there and wearing the hard hull cap. I did not see that at no time when I visited the dam. . . . I don't believe it was a act of God. It was a act of man."

Acts of Humanity

THE HISTORY OF COAL mining casts a long, ugly shadow. It is not a shadow many people see or care to know about. If confronted directly by it, the temptation would be strong to look *away* (recall that John F. Kennedy was shocked to see the poverty and misery of West Virginia communities that were but a short drive from the nation's capital). Appalachian residents are known to say that the destruction and degradation they daily endure would not be tolerated if it occurred near prosperous urban and suburban communities. After noting all the press coverage devoted to the *Exxon-Valdez* spill, one resident reported to me that Appalachian people must not be as cute as the sea otters suffering in Alaska. Another said that in the eyes of most Americans they had become "throwaway people."

In Appalachia, mountaintop-removal (MTR) mining has become the preferred method for extracting coal. MTR is the most destructive form of strip mining ever devised. If in previous times miners dug deeply into mountains to extract precious black seams, a dangerous and labor-intensive process, MTR blows up whole mountains to access the coal more efficiently and profitably.

Picture a mountain as an irregularly shaped piece of lasagna with multiple layers. The first coal layer is not on top. It may be several layers down. To get to it, basketball-size holes are drilled into the mountaintop, filled with a highly explosive mixture (the same ammonium nitrate and fuel oil mixture used by Timothy McVeigh to blow up the Oklahoma City Federal Building in 1995), and then detonated, sending layer after layer of vegetation, soil, and rock into creeks, streambeds, and valleys below. With the coal layer now exposed, heavy equipment can come in to easily and cheaply scoop it up.

The explosive process is then repeated to get to the next coal layer. The mountain gradually disappears, and the valleys around it slowly fill. Whole ecosystems simply vanish in this process. As one resident of Appalachia put it, "A deer crossing this land has got to pack a lunch."

It is difficult to imagine and appreciate the scope of the destruction caused by MTR. Southern Appalachia is home to two thousand species of flora, among them nearly eighty species of trees, making it one of the richest and most biologically diverse forests in the world. Some naturalists refer to it as the "rain forest of North America." Its mountains, some of the oldest in the world, with forests nearly three hundred million years old, now disappear in months. Numerous species of birds and animals can be found there. But in the wake of MTR, all this life, all this fertility and diversity and beauty, is reduced to rubble, a lifeless lunar landscape. Streams containing freshwater and fish are buried under mounds of the fill pushed off the mountain. When it rains, torrents of water readily become floods that destroy whatever lies in their path, because the vegetative and soil cover that would otherwise hold the rain has been wiped away. Groundwater and the trickles of streams that remain often run black and orange.

To bring some perspective to the issue, we need to compare the devastation happening in Appalachia to the gardening scene in Genesis. The Garden of Eden is presented as a fertile and fruitful place that inspires and supports life in all its diversity. That is why it is a place of delight. Though it may be inappropriate to make every place into a garden—some places will perhaps always be too wild to support the kind of domestication that gardening entails— the world is nonetheless at its best when fertility is nurtured and protected. The primordial vocation of humanity is to live in ways that contribute to the world's flourishing, because in doing so they participate in God's gardening ways with the world. Love wants all life to flourish.

It is hard to see how MTR is a participation in God's ongoing creating presence in the world. With effects ranging from defor- estation and water pollution to species eradication and ecosystem collapse, this manner of mining is a profoundly de-creative action. Though mining officials are quick to say that they return mined lands to their original contour and use, it is plain to knowledge- able observers that millions of years of evolutionary development— along with all the species diversity and ecosystem resilience this development produces—have been brought to a sudden and ugly halt. What may have once looked like a lush garden now resembles an unsightly, sickly scar.

The damage inflicted upon the land and wildlife of Appala- chia cannot be neatly separated from the damage inflicted upon its people. Once love is perverted and the power of sin becomes op- erative, it infiltrates all relationships. It creates a sick and wounded world that perpetuates itself and produces yet more pain and hurt. The logic that transforms creatures into commodities for profitable use is eventually applied to people as well.

The explosions that blow up mountains also destroy homes in the valleys below, cracking foundations and destroying water wells used for drinking, washing, and gardening. Sometimes they directly kill people, as happened in August 2004 when a massive boulder loosened by mining blasts rolled down a Virginia hillside crushing to death the sleeping three-year-old Jeremy Davidson. Coal dust is everywhere, and the noise of heavy machinery and explosions constant, making it difficult for people to be outside. Overloaded coal trucks speed through communities, destroying roads and making them unsafe for drivers and residents alike. In the spring of 2000, soon-to-be college graduate Darlies Carter was returning home from work when she was struck head-on and killed by an out-of-control, overloaded coal truck driven by a Xanax-intoxicated driver.

MTR functions according to an idolatrous economic logic that insists coal must be mined and produced at the lowest possible cost, even if that means land, water, people, and jobs are lost; in a little over twenty years, mining jobs in Kentucky were cut by nearly two-thirds, from approximately thirty-six thousand in 1979 to thirteen thousand in 2003. Coal companies claim that they are going to save Appalachia by providing jobs and making flat land available for industrial and recreational development. But as one resident put it to me, "It's a big lie that coal's gonna save Kentucky; coal hasn't saved us in a hundred damned years!" Coal counties are still among the poorest in the nation, while coal companies continue to be profitable. Today's coal production can't save Kentucky or West Virginia, because the current means of coal extraction destroys forests, watersheds, valleys, mountains, farms, gardens, and the families and communities they support.

The devastation being played out in southern Appalachia's coalfields is a witness to a sick heart and to the failure to love. It is true that agents of the destruction often claim to "love" their homelands—in some regions it is deemed unpatriotic to mount any criticism against coal-production practices—but as Kentucky writer Bob Sloan observes, these people are "moral midgets." They are like the men who beat their wives and girlfriends, sometimes sending them to the hospital multiple times, while professing how much they love them. "Mountaintop removal is the industrial equivalent of wife beating," says Sloan. "If you love a woman, you don't beat her. If you love a place, you don't allow it to be poisoned and polluted, gouged and leveled."[5]

PART IV

Redemption

CHAPTER 10

When Love Goes to Work, Life Is Healed

I came that they may have life, and have it abundantly.
JOHN 10:10

WHEN THE WORLD IS in trouble and life is being degraded or destroyed, the love of God goes to work in acts of healing. It responds by exposing and countering the counterfeit, corrupted forms of love that get in the way of genuine life. Love's desire, always, is that all creatures be well and attain the fullness of their being, which is why when creatures are wounded, love gets busy to bring about healing.

This fourth part of the book develops the many dimensions and ways of healing that love pursues. In particular, we must consider how healing changes the way we think about ourselves and engage in relationships and how healing takes place within contexts of communal life together. And we must think about the practices, like forgiveness, that repair and reinvigorate relationships that have fallen apart. All together, the diverse aspects of healing contribute to the work that Christians call *redemption*. It is work that leads to the world's salvation and flourishing. But first, some preliminary words about healing itself.

Healing is about much more than a more or less well function-ing body. That is because an individual functioning body, as impor-tant as that is, is only the visible tip of the much deeper phenomenon of health. The full realization of health encompasses minds, bodies, souls, and the vast array of relationships that join us to communi-ties and places. In order to appreciate the far-reaching dimensions of health, we must attend to the heart that is the animating core of our life as a whole.

Recall that when hearts are wounded or sick, people tend to turn *away* from others and then *inward* as a coping strategy. Protec-tive walls are built to keep the pain away. Healing, however, is the reverse movement; it is the action that *opens* people to others, the world, and to life's possibilities. It is the process whereby hearts are cleansed of fear and guilt and then redirected, so that people can participate in the flows of love that join them to each other, to their places, and to God. To be sick is to be dis-eased, ill at ease, unable to be with others in a harmonious way. It is, eventually, to find oneself fragmented and alone. To be healthy, on the other hand, is to be able to move freely, sympathetically, and shamelessly among others. It is to be able to experience the conviviality that is possible in a shared life. In Christian parlance, the name for the wholeness and joy of a healed life is *salvation*.

Put another way, when persons are healthy, the relationships that join them to communities and neighborhoods are life-giving and strong. Blessings are gratefully received, and help is gener-ously given. But when persons are sick, the relationships that would normally inspire and nurture them are broken, and the avenues of mutual care and delight cut off.

When health is understood in this expansive way, as strong and vigorous relationships *within* and *among* creatures, we can more readily appreciate why, from a Christian point of view, healing and forgiveness are so intimately connected. Forgiveness is the action that liberates people from the pain and guilt of their past, so that they can make a fresh start at living again. Without forgiveness a body can function just fine. The problem is that it will often function in the wrong sorts of ways. But with forgiveness a body, though perhaps injured or incapacitated, can still move in ways that bring joy and peace into the world. The difference between sickness and health depends on the strength of the love that is there at work. As the power of love increases, so too does the capacity to live.

It wasn't until I met Mark that I began to understand the deeper meaning of all this.

Healing as Transformation

SEVERAL YEARS AGO MARK Eddy and his family joined the small college community in Georgetown, Kentucky, where I worked. Wanting to help them feel welcome, my family had them over for dinner. Much to our delight, we discovered several shared interests and joys. I learned that Mark played bluegrass music. I hoped he would teach me to play the banjo. I even dreamed that we might someday form a little band and take the show to a stage.

But it was not to be. That first fall semester, Mark's years-long nagging cough got worse. It got so bad he could hardly cross his bedroom floor without stopping to catch his breath. Medical tests showed that he was in the advanced stages of cancer. He was told to call in his family, because he did not have long to live. Mark said that gathering his children around his bed to tell them he was soon going to die was the "worst moment of my life." We were all devastated.

Before joining our community, Mark had been working as a clinical therapist, but the work depressed him and made him unhappy. He didn't like himself or the people he served. Mark admitted he had become difficult to be around. He was so glad to be teaching college students now, because he felt he finally found work that was life-giving and life-fulfilling. Mark had come to feel more alive than he had in years. I could not imagine how he and his family would handle the cruel news of his terminal cancer.

It was evident to our church community that Mark's family would need a lot of help. Being new to the area, they had not yet had the time to establish deep networks of friendship and support. Nonetheless, major practical matters still had to be faced. How would his wife, Lisa, keep up in her new job as a middle-school teacher while attending to all of Mark's needs? How would his sons, Paul and Matt, make the transition into their new school while dealing with a father who was dying? Should Karen, their eldest child, leave college in Ohio to be with her family? Who would do the shopping, driving, cooking, and cleaning? Who would attend to Mark when family members were exhausted or beside themselves with grief?

It is remarkable to me that so many people made offers to help. Some brought food to the house. Some brought gift cards, so that the family could buy what they needed. Others volunteered to drop off and pick up the boys from school activities. Others committed to driving Mark to and from unending doctor's visits, thus freeing Lisa to do the work she simply needed to do. Some gave their time to sit with Mark, so he would not have to sit alone. People who barely knew the Eddys adopted them as their own family members, sharing food, sharing mistakes, sharing worry and fear, but also sharing hope. It was beautiful to see a community of love develop around this family. But it was also hard, because we each knew our own incompetence and doubt, our own selfishness and lack of faith. Seeing his family grieve, simply staying with each other during the months of ups and downs, watching a man slowly die, and knowing that our efforts to help were far from perfect—it was a lot to bear.

One Sunday morning not long before his death, Mark stood up before our congregation at Faith Baptist Church to bear witness to his life. He began by reading from a journal entry written several years before coming to be with us. Though physically "well" at that time, he was living a lonely hell:

> Or maybe all of this, the anxiety, the emptiness, the vague illnesses are all due to a common underlying factor: I dislike almost everything about my life, this town, this house, this job. They bore and disgust me. I have no friends and no group of people other than my family that I feel a part of, valued by, where I fit in. I dread getting up. If I am ever to be happy it will have to begin to happen soon. But I don't feel any closer to that goal than I was ten years ago.[1]

Mark described how he had been depressed for at least ten years. He was functioning physically, but hardly fully alive, because he was suffering from a sick heart. He described himself as sullen, withdrawn, angry, sad, and anxious. He didn't like people, and he didn't want them to like him. He was angry at God for not helping him. He gave up on God and became an atheist.

The healing of Mark's heart began with a psychiatrist who helped him understand his depression. Antidepressant drugs made it possible for him to see a little light in his world of darkness, enabling him to feel some love and happiness, but deep down he was still angry and anxious. He started to pray again. None of this was easy or simple, but gradually Mark began to see that God was calling him to leave his clinical work and restart his life as a college teacher. He saw that he needed to turn outward to help others, rather than remain locked within his own pain. That is when I came to know him.

When Mark stood before our congregation on September 24, 2006, he did so with an oxygen tank tucked under one arm. He said, "I feel better than I have felt in years. I can't thank God enough for that." But how could this be, given that he still had trouble breathing? The cancer was not gone. Yet Mark wanted to testify to a great miracle that had happened in his life. It was a miracle that liberated his soul and spirit from the lonely and anxious darkness that had gripped his life for years:

> When it became known that I was sick, I found myself surrounded by the light of love from people who hardly knew me. My family was flooded with prayers, food, cards, and the assurance that we were not alone and that others would be there for us. It was as though there were a thousand arms of love reaching out to us. And I knew it was the presence of God. I felt that I'd been overtaken by the kingdom of God and allowed briefly to look inside to experience just for a moment the love and joy of Christ's kingdom.

Mark had come to know himself as forgiven and newly empowered by the love of God as made real in the kindnesses of ordinary people. There were many years when he scarcely thought himself loveable. But now, the darkness and the pain of that past were forgiven. Love made it possible for him to be a father and a spouse dearly loved by his family. Love made him a valued friend in a new community, a friend who, though visibly dying, could be a source of encouragement and hope to people who had only recently come to know him. Mark could not have imagined that an ugly cancer would make his life and his world beautiful again.

One night while Mark was sleeping, Lisa looked over at him, thinking he might die at any moment. She wondered how she would manage without him. How would she handle watching him die? At that point Mark woke up, rolled over to her, and said, "I have never felt such joy and peace in all my life." They talked then about how God was making it possible for them to approach this terrible time with joy and peace. The anger and resentment that Mark had felt for years was gone, because he had been the beneficiary of a healing of heart, the sort of healing that freed him to see those around him as gifts from God. Filled with a love he had never known before, Mark said that God had cleansed his soul and wiped away the fear, anxiety, and hate that kept him in darkness. His spirit had been made new and reborn, so that the life he now lived could be animated by Christ's peace and joy and gentleness.

Mark ended his testimony to us with words from the prophet Isaiah: "The people who walked in darkness have seen a great light; those who lived in a land of darkness—on them light has shined" (9:2). He wanted us to know that God does not want any of us to be in loneliness and darkness. Jesus is the light of the world who has come to bring the abundance of life that is possible when love overtakes our hearts and minds. "This is what God has done for me. A light has blazed in my darkness. The healing light of Christ has blazed forth."

Jesus the Great Physician

THE GOSPELS REVEAL THAT the birth of Jesus was an occasion of such joy, because he was understood to be the one who would save people from the disordering sin and corrupting love that damages the world. Jesus is the savior expected by the prophets, because he brings healing to the whole world. He is the one who repairs relationships characterized by violence, injustice, and guilt and guides people into "the way of peace" (Luke 1:79).

Jesus came to be characterized as the great physician, because he understands so clearly how diseases develop and why relationships unravel. He diagnoses and cleanses sick hearts and then sets people free to live into a new life. Moreover, he models and invites people to share in forms of ministry that nurture, heal, and reconcile relationships. Looking to Jesus and then participating in the forms of life that he makes possible, we not only learn to see the nature of illness; we also discover possible and practical paths toward healing.

When John the Baptist asked Jesus who he was, Jesus responded by saying that because of him "the blind receive their sight, the lame walk, the lepers are cleansed, the deaf hear, the dead are raised, and the poor have good news brought to them" (Matt. 11:5). And when Jesus was getting ready to send his disciples out for the first time, he said, "As you go, proclaim the good news, 'The kingdom of heaven has come near.' Cure the sick, raise the dead, cleanse the lepers, cast out demons" (10:7–8). No wonder people came to him in droves. They wanted to see him and be addressed and touched by him, because they believed he had the power to heal their brokenness and lead them into a full and vital life.

The New Testament gospels are full of stories that show Jesus demonstrating the love that heals life. Jesus is proclaimed to be the savior of the world not because he plucks people out of this world—as if to relocate them in some ethereal, disembodied heaven—but because he performs the healing that enables them to experience life abundantly here and now.

To appreciate the wide scope of his healing presence, we can highlight several moments of Jesus's ministry as they are recorded in Luke's gospel. In these stories we can see that the healing Jesus performs, while clearly finding expression in the recovery of material bodies, extends to the cleansing of hearts, the freeing of souls, and the restoration of relationships. Above all we see Jesus respecting and restoring the dignity of individuals, so they can be participating members in the communities in which they live. People are "saved" because they are given the fresh opportunity to experience the wholeness of life. Jesus never simply sees people only in the wounded conditions they presently find themselves in: lonely, ostracized, maimed, out of their minds, or dead. Instead, he sees what their lives could be if their suffering was healed.

One day while Jesus was preaching in a synagogue, a crippled, bent-over woman approached him. She had not been able to stand up straight for eighteen years. Jesus called her over, laid his hands on her, and she immediately stood up straight. Jesus said, "Woman, you are set free from your ailment" (Luke 13:12).

While traveling through the country of the Gerasenes, Jesus encountered a naked demon-possessed man who made his home among the tombs. Visibly unwell and distraught, he was a danger to himself and to others. Area residents had unsuccessfully tried to bind him with shackles and chains. He broke the chains each time and fled into the wilds. Jesus commanded the demons to depart from him, which they did by entering into a herd of swine. No longer living among and like the dead, the man became calm and returned to his right mind (Luke 8:26–39).

Upon returning from this trip, Jesus encountered a crowd of people who had been waiting for him. In the crowd was a woman who had been suffering from a hemorrhage for twelve years. She had spent all the money she had on doctors, but none could cure her. Unnoticed, she approached Jesus from behind, touched the fringe of his clothes, and her bleeding stopped immediately (Luke 8:43–48).

Aware of Jesus's healing power, a synagogue leader named Jairus emerged from the crowd and begged Jesus to come to his house because his only daughter was dying. But it was too late. Jairus received word that his daughter had just died. Upon hearing the news, Jesus said, "Do not fear. Only believe, and she will be saved" (Luke 8:50). Jesus went to Jairus's house, took the daughter's hand, and asked her to get up. To the astonishment of everyone there, the girl got up at once.

While traveling through a city Jesus met a man with leprosy who begged to be made clean (in that society uncleanness, or lack of ritual purity, was considered grounds for social ostracism). The leper told Jesus that it was within his power to make him well, for in being made clean he would be able to rejoin his community. Jesus touched him, and immediately the leprosy left him (Luke 5:12–13).

One day when Jesus was teaching, some men came carrying a paralyzed man on a bed. They couldn't get through the door because there were so many people, so they lowered him through the roof. Jesus was impressed by the love of the men for this paralyzed man, and it was by their faith that Jesus could help him. Jesus said, "Friend, your sins are forgiven you" (Luke 5:20). Religious leaders were upset that Jesus presumed to forgive this man's sins (they believed that only God can forgive). As a sign that he had the authority to forgive, Jesus then ordered the man to stand up and walk. He did.

These stories, among many others, are clear demonstrations of Jesus's healing power. So many people came from so many directions—all of them bringing with them the wounds of their bodies and their worlds—because he represented a compassionate and empowering response to life's suffering. "They had come to hear him and to be healed of their diseases; and those who were troubled with unclean spirits were cured. And all in the crowd were trying to touch him, for power came out from him and healed all of them" (Luke 6:18–19).

It is right to call these acts of healing miracles. People were surprised and astounded by Jesus's ability to transform sickness and death into new life. We should be clear, however, about what it means to call his work a "miracle." For many people a miracle is an interruption or an abrogation of the laws of nature. Bodies "naturally" get sick and die because their physiology demands it. If sickness and death are overcome at the mere word or touch of Jesus, that must be a sign that Jesus has reversed or canceled what would have otherwise happened.

It is a mistake to interpret Jesus's miracles as "interruptions" in the world. They are better understood to be focal moments in which Jesus shows us creatures as they are meant by God to be: physically healthy, well fed, of right mind, and in right relationship with each other. As such, miracles are God making right something within the world that has gone wrong. That means miracles are not an *interruption* in the life of creatures, but rather those creatures' *liberation* to move into the life that God desires for them. Sickness, hunger, demon possession, guilt, alienation—these are all forms of degradation that damage and hurt creatures, forms that prevent creatures from becoming who they really are. Miracles make right what has, for whatever reason, gone wrong. When Jesus heals life, he reveals what life was meant to be all along. In his own life of love he reveals that the fullness of a human life is only achieved in the activation of love.

Jesus enters into the world's brutality and needless suffering and shows them not to be "natural" at all. Illness, hunger, derangement, injustice, hostility—these are all reflections of creation having gotten off course. Miracles are, therefore, God's "no" to all the forces in this life that undermine and wound creatures. And they are God's "yes" to life's freshness and vitality, God's "yes" to all the possibilities that creatures can realize if they are no longer shackled by the evil that stifles, distorts, and demeans life. Miracles are focal moments that remind us of God's continuing creative power.

How is Jesus able to do this? Christianity is founded upon the stupendous claim that Jesus of Nazareth is the embodied realization of the divine love that creates and nurtures all life. Jesus is God's eternal love precisely and personally focused and made fully active in the world. His movements are the love of God going to work. Because Jesus is believed to be God in the flesh, that means he is our window into what God the Creator most desires for all of creation. To see Jesus is to see what human life at its best can be. To encounter his body is to meet a person wholly and only animated by divine love. This why to be touched by Jesus is also to be touched by the power that creates and sustains the universe. Jesus is God fully entering into our pain and wounds, working to transform them from within. Jesus is God living our questions, frustrations, and struggles. Jesus is God creating new life in the midst of brokenness. Jesus is God physically embracing the torn fabric of our lives, working to mend and make beautiful the tapestry of creation.

It is precisely because Jesus is the embodied expression of God's creating love that he can also be creation's healer. He knows, we might say, "from the inside" what creatures need to thrive, because he opened himself fully to the depth of human experience. Upon encountering a creature, Jesus sees the wounds and brokenness that mar and distort life, but he is not limited by this vision of wounds. He also sees the full potential of what or who is there. He fully recognizes each creature as the embodied expression of God's love and thus understands what each creature needs so that it can maximally express the creative, nurturing love that leads to life's fullness and abundance.

Jesus is understood by Christians to be the great healer of life because in him we see the *reason* and the *agency* through which all life is said to be created. In him we see why anything was created in the first place and what its ultimate purpose is. John's gospel put it this way: Jesus is the creative word (*logos*) through whom all things come to be and the center through whom all things circulate. "All things came into being through him, and without him not one thing came into being. What has come into being in him was life" (1:3–4). Not just mere existence, but life in all its fullness and abundance. Jesus is said to be "the way, the truth, and the life" (14:6), because he puts life on a new path that leads creatures into healing, life-giving communion with others and with God. He is "the light of life" (1:4–5) because he both reveals what gets in the way of life's fulfillment and is himself the model of and the way toward the achievement of life at its best. "I came that they may have life, and have it abundantly" (10:10).

If Jesus is the embodiment of the love that creates and animates the whole world, then we as creatures in this world are fulfilled insofar as we learn to live through this love. And living in the flow of this love we experience the joys of a healthy life.

CHAPTER 11

The Communal Contexts of Health

We know that we have passed from death to life
because we love one another.
1 JOHN 3:14

A HEALTHY INDIVIDUAL IS, IN certain respects, a contradiction in terms. By this I mean that a person cannot be healthy *alone*. As we have already seen, to live as a creature is to live through the nurture that others provide. Though we might like to think of ourselves as self-standing, self-making individuals, the truth is that we could not stand at all, were it not for the fact that mothers birth us, creatures feed us, communities raise us, teachers inspire us, and friends comfort and correct us. Life is not simply lived *with* or *alongside* others. It is lived *through* others and *by means of* them. This is why it is so important to learn to live in community with others. In this chapter we develop an appreciation for the communal contexts of health.

A healthy and flourishing life is always life *together*. That means we have to think differently about what life is and how it happens and thrives. We need fresh ways to conceive what a human being *in relation to others* looks like.

Jesus once asked his followers to think of life as a massive vine with innumerable branches. Each person, he said, is like a branch that exists only because it is connected to the vine that supports and nourishes it. The branch does not choose whether it will be attached, because without attachment it can be and do nothing. Its only choice is if it will accept the nurture that the vine provides. If it does, then the branch will grow and eventually produce beautiful leaves and delicious fruit.

Jesus says he is the vine and his Father is the vine grower. He says that the life of the whole plant is the effect of the action of love circulating through all of its parts. The vine exists only because God the Father loves it, and each branch exists only because Jesus the Son loves it. Each branch, therefore, must learn to abide in Jesus, because when it does, it will be open to receive and extend the love that flows through him. By abiding in the love of Jesus, people will discover in themselves the joy of life that is in Jesus and so find that their own joy is made complete (John 15:1–11). The key to a full and abundant life is not only to be connected to others, but to have the love of God moving among and through us all. Love is the energy that holds the life of the vine together.

This striking image communicates the seamlessness of life. Our life is not an assemblage of various parts whose coming together is optional or haphazard. Rather, we are bound together in an organic fashion, each one of us joined to others through innumerable vascular channels that circulate the nutrients of life. In a plant's life, no element is insignificant or wasted. Leaves, though receiving food from the vine's roots, also open to the sunlight to receive its energy and then transport it back into the vine. Trunks' roots sink deep into the ground, where they are in complex conversation with water, minerals, and the billions of microorganisms that promote plant resilience and flourishing. A plant isn't an object, static and discretely determined. It is more like a process that grows by being in sympathetic and nurturing relationship with soil, water, air, and light. If at any moment one element of the plant, say a particular leaf, tries to extricate itself from the process, it will simply wilt and die. If enough elements fail to contribute, the whole plant dies, along with all the fruit and flowers it promised to the world. The dissolution of love, in other words, leads to the dissolution of life.

After giving his disciples this image, Jesus commands them to love each other with the same kind of love that he has demonstrated in his life. They are to lay down their lives for each other (John 15:12–13). This is a strange way of speaking. What could it mean to lay down one's life for another? I think Jesus is asking his followers to make their lives conduits of love. As we saw earlier in the example of Brother Luc, he is saying that they are to consider themselves channels through which his nurturing and healing power can flow into others. They are, in a manner of speaking, to become like xylem cells in a plant, which transport water and mineral elements from the ground up, and phloem cells, which transport organic compounds like sucrose from the sun-drenched leaves down. They are, in other words, to live together in such a way that they form a circulatory system that nourishes each member with the elements of love: kindness, attention, humility, service, celebration. And to do that, they have to come close to each other, cell touching cell, membrane lying next to membrane, so that the love that makes their joy complete can spread far and wide.

This picture of human life and flourishing is jarring, especially when considering how much pride people take in distinguishing themselves from the rooted life of a lowly plant. But it communicates what a great mistake it is to think that human beings exist as self-standing, unencumbered individuals. We are joined to each other, cell touching cell, altogether dependent on the nurture that flows throughout the whole matrix of tissue and flesh that is our life. Though we each exist as individual persons, our identity and agency are entirely dependent on how well we are able to fully face each other, receiving the nurture we need and giving the help we are uniquely equipped to provide. When the love of Jesus is found to be circulating among people, they are enabled to face each other with care and without shame.

When the apostle Paul looked for an image to communicate the sort of life that Jesus makes possible, he too went with an organic metaphor: a living body. Writing to the church at Corinth, he says that persons each have gifts of some sort, gifts that make them who they uniquely are. The mistake people make is in thinking that the gifts that *distinguish* individuals are the basis for creating a *separation* between individuals. A living body has many members—hands, feet, eyes, lungs, stomach, and so on—but none can function apart from the shared life of the whole (1 Cor. 12:12–26). The key to a successful and flourishing life is for each member to acknowledge and be sensitive to the distinct value of each other member, even when that member is unseen or distantly connected. This is why prayer is so important in the life of faith. Prayer is the regular action that opens people to others and to God. It is the art that trains us to perceive with honesty and detailed attention the many ways our lives are enfolded within the lives of others, and it is the disposition that then enables us to move gratefully and responsibly among them.

This image of the body again points out the fallacy of the conception of people as self-standing individuals. For any member of the body to be at its best, all other members must be at their best too. The moment dispositions like arrogance, negligence, boredom, or fear enter into the membership, the body as a whole and each of its members begin to suffer. As persons we rely on each other for daily support and encouragement. *Every* member matters, even the one who may not appear to be important. In a thriving body, no member should feel unwanted or insecure: "But God has so arranged the body, giving the greater honor to the inferior member, that there may be no dissension within the body, but the members may have the same care for one another. If one member suffers, all suffer together with it; if one member is honored, all rejoice together with it" (1 Cor. 12:24–26).

Paul is clear that the great danger is the emergence of division and dissension between people, which will keep them from being healthy or thriving. Rather than living into the future with confidence and enjoying the support of others, people can't succeed because they are worried they will be cut down or left alone. But equally important, when the gifts of others are not appreciated and developed, the whole body suffers. We need each other to help discover, unleash, and develop in each other the gifts that, when made active, will take the body as a whole to new possibilities. A community that is the "body of Christ" will be a membership of mutual encouragement, instruction, service, and celebration.

Imagine for a moment what your life would be like if the people you knew were each devoted to helping you find and then exercise your gifts, thereby helping you realize all that is best in your life. Then imagine yourself being that sort of person too, and all of you working for the good of each other and the whole community. This is what Paul is looking for. It is the sort of life that he thinks Jesus makes possible. He calls it life in Christ or life in the Holy Spirit.

None of this is easy. When people do manage to come together, actually live together, it seems that jealousy, spite, or boredom, among many other divisive dispositions, eventually develops. As a species we seem to be particularly adept at injuring each other. Living in particular cultures, we are each shaped by histories of racism, sexism, and various other forms of oppression. And so we come to a most important question: If a healthy life is always life together, what, practically speaking, are the forms and ways of life we need to learn, so that our presence is nurturing and healing? What does it take to make a vibrant community of healthy persons?

Opening into Community

COMMUNITY BEGINS WHEN PEOPLE open themselves to the lives of others and then allow themselves to be changed by what they discover. It means putting aside the blinders that enable us to move through our neighborhoods mostly oblivious to what is really going on. To be in communion with others, you have to truly notice them, get close, stay for a while, learn, and eventually gain enough trust, so that they feel comfortable communicating the truth of what is happening in their lives. Only then is it possible for you to determine together what can be done that would be of mutual help.

To see what I mean, consider the story of Eunice, a young woman in Kenya. Like millions of women around the world, her life has been extremely hard. She easily falls within the group of people considered by some to be too insignificant to merit notice, let alone attention.

Our story begins when Eunice, the youngest of twelve children, left her village to travel to Nairobi, where she hoped to get a job and start a new life. While on the bus, Eunice enjoyed a conversation with a man in which she told him her story and shared with him her dreams of her future life. He seemed nice enough. Her aunt was supposed to meet her at the bus station and help connect her with her sister. When the aunt failed to come, the man offered to take Eunice to his home to spend the night. He then raped her and threatened to kill her if she told anyone.

Three months later, having returned home and showing signs of pregnancy, Eunice had to tell her family what happened. Her father was furious. He broke Eunice's mother's arms. He threatened to kill Eunice and her mother if Eunice continued to live in the village. Eunice left again, hoping that her departure would restore some peace to her mother's life.

Eunice returned to Nairobi, but did not know what she was

going to do. She tried to abort her child, but failed in the attempt. A hospital doctor gave her the encouragement she needed by saying that the baby she was carrying was a blessing. Though she had nearly nothing in the way of economic means to raise the child, she trusted that God would provide for her and her child:

> By the grace of God, I delivered my son without complications. I didn't have any clothes to dress him after birth, but only the scarf I bought. When I told the doctors the whole story, they gave me money to buy food. My son and I left for our home early in the morning. After three days, I had to leave my child in the house to search for money. I went to where I used to wash clothes and was given a job. I was in a lot of pain, but had no option but to work. I continued living like that until my child grew up.

Over the following years Eunice put together various part-time jobs to make meager ends meet. She was working so that she could afford her son's education and take care of her mother, who had always helped her. Eventually, and with the kind help of a few others, Eunice was able to enroll at the university herself. She showed up in class with dirty feet and dirty teeth.

This is where we need to pause in the story. Eunice is one face among countless others. It would be easy to see her and not think twice about her life. But behind her face is a story of immense struggle and pain. The world is full of faces like that. To be sure, their stories may not all be tales of rape and abandonment, but all people carry wounds within themselves, wounds that prevent them from flourishing and fully contributing to the lives around them. For many, the thought of revealing personal stories of pain and struggle and failure is terrifying. "What would people think if they knew the truth about me?" It is a lot easier to hide behind, "I'm fine. How about you?" The result is that we move within a social world of concealed and unknown wounds. And because life is busy for most everyone, it is a lot easier to stick to yourself, not ask questions, and assume that the people we meet are okay.

But if no one stops to notice and engage, people like Eunice will be left to their own struggles. They will remain alone, living a withering, wilted existence. The gifts that are uniquely theirs will remain undeveloped, and the life of their neighborhoods impoverished.

The flowering of communion life depends on people opening themselves to each other so that pain can be addressed and promise unleashed. It requires that we resist the anonymity, stereotypes, and prejudices that otherwise come so easily to us. Only then can a community and its individual members truly flourish.

The healing of a wounded world is the heart of the good-news life that Christians are called to live. Christians become members of the church, so that they can learn to open themselves and relate to each other and the world in ways that continue and extend Jesus's healing presence. Here they learn that the care of self is inseparable from the care of others and that the primary task is to put the love of God to work in the world. Church is the place where people learn to attend to the needs of others and then practice the skills of nurture, healing, and reconciliation. They learn to swim in the flow of God's love, so that they can channel and apply that love wherever they might be.

Admittedly, Christians have often failed in their calling. They have frequently been blind to the pain around them and have sought their own comfort and security. Like many others, Christians are often frightened by the prospect of being changed by what they see. After all, opening oneself up to the pain of another and then allowing oneself to be transformed by that pain is so daunting, because the result is that one may have to live a very different life than the one first planned. Think, for a moment, of how difficult it is for people to confront their own racism, learn to appreciate and affirm

the lives of people they were once prejudiced against, and then attempt to live in beloved community with them.

But this is precisely what Jesus did: in love he opened himself
completely to the suffering of others, took all the world's violence
and wounds within himself, and then responded with the power
that heals and restores. Love does not seek to be immune from pain.
It goes to work within it. Love is the power that is uniquely sympathetic and responsive to the suffering that is going on around. Love's
point of view does not accept the abandonment of even one person
to pain. Love takes the position of a caring shepherd who, despite
having ninety-nine sheep that are safe, still searches the wilderness
for the one sheep that is lost (Luke 15:3–7).

In Jesus we see most clearly that the love that creates and nurtures the world is also the love that heals it. In him we learn that it
would be a contradiction for love to create but not to heal, because
the logic of love is to want the beloved to flourish. Whatever gets in the
way of a creature's thriving is an affront to God's good and beautiful
creation and therefore also an assault on God's love.

We can now resume our story of Eunice with the introduction
of Marion.[1] Marion met Eunice through her sister, a classmate of
Eunice's. The tremendous pain and need behind Eunice's beautiful
smile was obvious to Marion. What should she do? She began by
taking Eunice to a store and buying personal items like soap, laun-
dry detergent, body lotion, toothpaste, and toothbrushes for Eunice
and her now four-year-old son.

But toothpaste and a toothbrush could only be a beginning step.
When Marion returned home after this meeting, she could not get
Eunice out of her mind. "I sat and thought and asked myself, 'How
sustainable is that?' Even if I bought her a toothbrush, she needs
more than a toothbrush. And how long is that toothpaste going
to last?" Marion had opened her heart to Eunice, and the experience moved her deeply. She saw that there were many more young
women in Kenya like Eunice who were hurting and who suffered

from broken promises, sexual assault, rejection by family, and physical and verbal abuse. Marion needed to do something about it. She needed to find practical ways to share the love of Jesus.

She told her friend Nikole Lim, a young Asian American filmmaker, about Eunice. Nikole had been working on a documentary film called *While Women Weep,* which featured the stories of women around the world who were turning personal hardship into triumph. Researching for the film, Nikole came across disturbing statistics: poor women do not have access to essential resources and the education they need to survive; young girls struggling to pay rent and feed their families are often forced into prostitution as the only way to finance living expenses; rape is common; rape victims are often kicked out of school or forced out of family homes for being pregnant; many girls attempt self-induced abortions with chlorine intoxication, birth-control pill overdoses, or knitting needles and metal wires; one in five of these young women dies in the attempt.

When Marion told Nikole about Eunice's situation, Nikole sent $350 to cover the expenses of the school term. This scholarship enabled Eunice to focus on her studies, rise to the top of her class, and graduate with a degree in psychology and counseling. Now, several years after her own rape, Eunice wants to be a counselor for girls who have been victims of sexual assault, a marvelous testimony to the truth that when people invest in helping others discover and realize their talents, even those people once thought not to have talents worth developing, the whole world benefits.

Learning about Eunice and the pain of millions of other girls around the world, Nikole also realized she could not simply walk away. "God was tugging at my heart, challenging me to be a voice for those who are silenced by oppression. I then heard the voice of God asking me, 'Nikole, now that you have seen the brokenness of women in Africa, what are you going to do about it?'" Nikole understood how easy it is to be afraid of the pain that is going on around her. But she also knew that it is only by opening herself to others that she can genuinely find her life as one of communion *with* others. The struggles and the successes of others were becoming sources of insight and inspiration to her, helping her see what needed doing and how she could help. But the weight of the world's suffering was also showing her how risky and painful it can be to give one's life to the world's need. It is so much easier to focus on yourself. Nikole says:

> Through Eunice's story, I was liberated from my own selfishness. As God was challenging my heart, I felt called to start an organization to provide spiritual, educational, and economic empowerment for girls worldwide. I thought that maybe God was calling me to be a part of something greater—a part of stories that could change not only my life, but the lives of many other women who are vulnerable to sexual abuse.

Nikole discovered her vocation to lead people into the embrace of God's love and to testify to that love as the power that enables people to weave their lives into each other:

> Through this process of working to advocate for those in oppression, God has been conforming my heart to feel the joys and pains of His. Daily, I hear stories of suffering, despair, and brokenness. I meet people who are crying desperately for help. It breaks my heart knowing there are so many others who have not yet felt the embrace of God's love and compassion. I only hope to fulfill God's purpose for me by being an activator of His love and compassion by leveraging stories of dignity through the ministry of Freely in Hope.

Inspired by the struggles and the hope of women like Eunice, Marion and Nikole had created Freely in Hope, an organization devoted to helping women combat poverty and oppression by providing opportunities for education, counseling, and economic development. As Marion puts it, "Freely in Hope started with a toothbrush and toothpaste." But its goal is to lift women out of poverty and limit the vulnerability caused by sexual abuse. Its mission statement reads: "Freely in Hope is dedicated to restoring justice, dignity, and hope by liberating women and their families from the bondages of poverty. Our vision is for women worldwide to experience God's transformative love by living freely in hope."

Freely in Hope is a small organization, but it is a big witness to the love of God that builds communion and therefore also the conditions for a flourishing life. The work of healing young women who have faced so much abuse and pain is not easy. It takes time to understand the story of each person so that appropriate help can be provided. It takes patience to appreciate and confront the fears that keep people from fully realizing their potential. It takes commitment to develop the practical skills and networks of support that will carry these women daily on their paths toward self-respect and resilience.

These women who have been rejected by society need to learn to love themselves and know God as the one who loves them at every moment. They need to rebuild their lives from what are often ruins. They need to be able to tell their own stories, clarify their own emotions, and by sharing their lives begin the process of healing. Telling their stories to others, being able to narrate obstacles faced and overcome, is a practical demonstration of the power of love to heal and inspire. Knowing they are embraced by people cheering them on and willing to help them gives them the courage they need to move forward. Healing and hope are born in places like this.

Freely in Hope partners with other organizations to help these women learn a trade or skill or start their own business. Some have opened a small salon or restaurant. The organization encourages these women to identify their calling in life and then helps them take the steps to achieve their goals. Success is measured by the ability of these women to realize their potential and thus more fully become themselves. Marion says, "We do not impose decisions or choices on them. We discuss together the choices. The girls have their own minds, and they know better what they want to do with their lives."

The name for Freely in Hope comes from Matthew's gospel: "Freely you have received; freely give" (10:8, NIV). But the inspiration comes from Luke 4:18–19, where Jesus, quoting the prophet Isaiah, announces his own ministry: "The Spirit of the Lord is upon me, because he has anointed me to bring good news to the poor. He has sent me to proclaim release to the captives and recovery of sight to the blind, to let the oppressed go free, to proclaim the year of the Lord's favor."

Freely in Hope seeks to enable people to participate in God's healing love in the world. It is a Christian "school" for the learning of love. This love is not an abstraction or a vague feeling. It is a practical, social, and economic force that inspires and empowers people to knit themselves into the lives of others, so that together they can create a more resilient and beautiful world. Through sharing life together—sharing meals, skills, fears, dreams, work—people become stronger and better than when they are left alone.

But to come together, it is essential that we first break down barriers of ignorance and overcome patterns of negligence that keep us separated from each other. Healing can happen when we know that others care for us and are willing to help us in times of struggle and pain. Healing can happen when we live together, because it is our proximity to each other, the fact that we daily share life's disappointments and opportunities, fears and excitements, that enables us to help, encourage, and celebrate each other.

Nikole says that as she finds herself broken by the wounds of others, and when she brings these wounds and her own brokenness to Jesus, he completes her with stories that transform and restore her.

The mercy and compassion Jesus shows going to the cross and the power he reveals in his resurrection from the dead inspire her with the hope that, despite all the world's brutality, the power of love is stronger than violence. "There is beauty in the broken," she says.[2]

Staying Together

IT IS ONE THING to open yourself to others and come alongside to be with them. It is quite another to stay with them over the long haul. To do that you have to come to terms with the fact that they will eventually irritate and disagree with you and that you will annoy and hurt them too. No matter how well-meaning people are, the fact is that individuals are different and sometimes difficult to be with. Each of us, simply by being ourselves, will pursue paths that eventually collide with others' and produce tension, conflict, and hurt. We will be tempted to walk away or build up walls of isolation and protection, which is why it is so important that we learn and appreciate what it takes to *stay together*. As we will soon see, the practice of forgiveness plays a central role in the art of staying together.

One way to characterize our problem is to say that we often desire to be in relationship with an idea of a person rather than with the person as he or she really is. We want the individual to conform to our image of that person. To see what I mean, consider the following scenario, one that centers on the prospects of romantic love.

Imagine going to a party where you meet a person you think could be a good friend, perhaps even a life partner. You begin to see each other regularly and generally have a good time. You share similar interests and hobbies, and you regularly agree in your conversations about politics. It starts to dawn on each of you that you'd like to get married, since you bring such happiness to each other.

But you have also started to notice that the other does little things that really annoy you: he is not as neat and tidy as you thought he would be; she spends money on items you consider questionable; he keeps repeating sports stories from the glory days of his youth; she asks questions that make you wonder if she really trusts you; he acts like a control freak in areas you consider none of his business; she loves to present herself as the victim; he has behaviors you think are neurotic. Of course, this is only a partial list. But the point is that you are beginning to see that your beloved is not quite who you thought he or she was. Your beloved has weaknesses, makes mistakes, and acts on habits you find bothersome. The characteristics you dislike are not new. They are, rather, freshly revealed to you because you now have had the time to get to know your beloved more deeply and more honestly. Your idea of the beloved is being challenged by the truth of who he or she really is. What will you do?

One strategy is to snipe and bicker and to suggest that your "beloved" is the one with all the problems. This strategy is a perennial favorite because it takes you off the hook. You can be the superior one who stands in judgment. You can be the one who points out all the flaws in another and elevate yourself to the status of savior, as the one who is beyond judgment. All blame for the relationship, all blame for your own frustration and failure, can now be placed at the feet of the other. It is all very convenient.

Another strategy is to become a victim yourself. You are the one who is getting a bad deal out of this relationship. You had no idea that your "beloved" would turn out to be so objectionable, so neurotic. And so you retreat into yourself, begin to act more and more like a disinterested roommate, and pine for the day when you will find a means of escape. You begin to look at other people, secretly believing that if only you could be with one of them, your life would be so much better. You are not going to talk it through or fight. It is too much effort. The two of you slowly grow more and more apart.

Of course, other strategies exist, but we have enough to see that there is a great deal of deception and dishonesty in all of this. The temptation is to assume that the problems and the fault lie elsewhere. We love to be right. And if we don't hold the power, we love to be the innocent victim. But is any one of us always right or fully innocent? Chances are that if members of the relationship were to commit to honest and sustained conversation—a possibility not to be taken for granted—both would discover how they carry within themselves variations of the behavior they find objectionable in the other. It is easy to claim that the other is the neurotic one. It is painful to admit one's own neuroses. It can be devastating to acknowledge about oneself the many weaknesses, hurts, fears, arrogance, and insecurity (the list goes on and on) that prevent us from standing before each other without shame.

Without trying to, without knowing it, we can be inattentive, indifferent, or hurtful. We'd be much better off if we acknowledged that each of us enters into relationships already bearing many wounds, so we ought to be more merciful with ourselves and with each other. But mercy comes hard. Whether out of insecurity or spite, it is often easier to be hard on each other.

So much of our inability to love others and to stay with them stems from an inability to love ourselves properly. When we are with others and honest about the discoveries we make about them and ourselves, we realize that we are each flawed in unique ways, depending on the history each person has lived through. When we are attentive, it is plain that each of us can be as negligent, petty, and arrogant as the next person. Add to that a need to self-protect and self-promote and you have all the makings of what can easily be considered an unattractive and unlovable being. But when people believe themselves to be unlovable and unlovely, should we expect them to be able to love someone else? And so we come to a surprising conclusion: the nature of life together and the acknowledgment of our failures at trying to be with others reveal how unlovable we each can be. Now that's depressing!

Actually, it is entirely liberating, provided we understand that the love-worthiness of people is not dependent on how blameless they are. From a Christian point of view, you don't have to be perfect to be loved, which is a remarkably good thing, since none of us can go through an entire life without screwing up in some way.

The apostle Paul put it this way. After noting that "all have sinned and fall short of the glory of God" (Rom. 3:23), he then goes on to say, "But God proves his love for us in that while we still were sinners Christ died for us" (5:8). In other words, God knows fully and truly the depths of all our shame and wrongdoing, but that does not prevent God from loving us and giving himself completely and sacrificially to us. What makes us lovable is not what we have done or might yet do. We are lovable because God creates us. As children of God, we are each the embodied expression of divine love. God wants to see every creature attain the fullness of its life. We are, therefore, called to love ourselves and each other because God first loves us.

And the love God shows, as we have already said, is tenacious: "For I am convinced that neither death, nor life, nor angels, nor rulers, nor things present, nor things to come, nor powers, nor height, nor depth, nor anything else in all creation, will be able to separate us from the love of God in Christ Jesus our Lord" (Rom. 8:38–39). This is liberation, to know that no matter what shameful things you have experienced or will yet do, God will continue to love you. Jesus's ministries to everyone and his association with society's outcasts show that you can be a complete and utter scoundrel, and God will still welcome you, be hospitable to you, and then invite you to extend that same love to others.

Another way to state God's love for us it to say that God forgives. Forgiveness is an essential movement within love's communal way of life. Forgiveness liberates people from the shame and misery that otherwise would keep them in contention with others or locked within the private, lonely hells they create. Together with confession and repentance, forgiveness opens the door for us to be merciful with ourselves and with each other. It creates the space in which we can admit our shame, make amends, turn to others, and say, "Let's try again."

Forgiveness is not easy, especially if the person you need to forgive is difficult or hurts you. But it is essential, because forgiveness liberates people from the many strategies that keep them locked in self-pity or self-righteousness. Forgiveness enables people to step out of their own pain, so that they can embrace others again. And repentance alerts others that we have given up on the strategies of self-righteousness. When we confess, repent, and forgive each other, we acknowledge that none of us are perfect and that we each need each other to make life better.

Forgiveness is not contingent upon whether the person to be forgiven is worthy of it. If that were the prerequisite, no one would be forgivable, because everyone has wronged another. And if no one is forgivable, then everyone is locked within a life-denying world of guilt and retribution. Paul reminds us, "*All* have sinned and fall short of the glory of God."

In the Lord's Prayer Jesus instructs his followers to daily ask for and grant forgiveness; it is the discipline that enables us to stick with others even when they have hurt us and we have hurt them. If people are to be able to come together and stay together, remembering that it is only as we live together in communion that the fullness of personal life can be achieved, a capacity for trust must develop, so we can honestly speak to each other about how we have wronged and been wronged. Put another way, the sign of a healthy relationship is one in which I can ask you, "What have I done that requires me to ask for forgiveness?" When the person wounded can speak honestly and I do not become defensive or run away, a path is opened for mutual healing to begin. The name of this path is forgiveness, and its destination is mutual delight.

The Ritual Forms of Communal Life

A LIFE OF COMMUNION and forgiveness doesn't just happen, especially if you find yourself lonely or surrounded by people who have little regard for community. To live a healthy life people need the support of each other, and they need ritual practices that remind them of and keep them focused on fundamental commitments and goals. Early Christians understood this, which is why they instituted two essential practices for communion life: baptism and the Eucharist. Baptism signifies a person's cleansing and entrance into community, and the Eucharist is the regular meal that nurtures people in the ways of love. Think of these ritual practices as learning exercises or apprenticeship disciplines in the school of love.

Those who wanted to become followers of Jesus, and thus also participants in his healing ways with the world, soon learned that following him presupposed a transformed imagination. They could not simply join in with him if their imaginations and hearts were not themselves first healed. Jesus put it starkly: "If any want to become my followers, let them deny themselves and take up their cross daily and follow me. For those who want to save their life will lose it, and those who lose their life for my sake will save it" (Luke 9:23–24).

Jesus is pointing to the fact that the many forms of wounding we experience in life have the effect of turning us inward and making us worry or obsess about ourselves. When we spend much of our time wondering if we are pretty enough, capable enough, rich enough, good enough—all anxious questions reflecting insecurity about our own worth—we invariably focus our energy and act in ways that aim to put ourselves above or ahead of others. Without being malicious about it, we make ourselves the center of attention. Put on this self-serving path, we end up bringing harm to ourselves and to others. And so Jesus says his followers must deny themselves. They must be willing to lose themselves, because it is as they forget that they are the center of the universe that others can become the focus of their attention and celebration.

The self-denial that Jesus is talking about has nothing to do with self-loathing. Why? Because each creature is the material manifestation of God's love and thus the focus of God's delight. No creature is worthy of loathing. Jesus instructs his followers to deny themselves, because he understands how an improper self-love gets in the way of the true love that welcomes and nurtures others. When people make themselves the center of the universe, they actually undermine the possibility of personal well-being and happiness. Improper self-love gets in the way of shared life together.

This is why those wanting to be followers of Jesus need to undergo a "baptism" of their hearts and minds. They need to go through a discernment process in which they uncover the dimensions of false love, see how this false love is at work within themselves, and then make the commitment to love properly. The apostle Paul described this process in memorable language: "We know that our old self was crucified with him so that the body of sin might be destroyed, and we might no longer be enslaved to sin. For whoever has died is freed from sin. But if we have died with Christ, we believe that we will also live with him" (Rom. 6:6–8). In baptism corrupted love is exorcised and the degrading forms of relating to others are put to death, so that we can be a blessing to each other. It is as if one enters the ocean of God's love, is cleansed, and emerges clean and new.

With baptism the look of the world and of life are changed, because one's point of view has been altered. Paul put it this way: "So if anyone is in Christ, there is a new creation: everything old has passed away; see, everything has become new!" (2 Cor. 5:17). Everything has become new because every creature is now perceived through the optic of the divine love that cherishes everything and everyone. Rather than seeing creatures as a threat or objects of idolatry or envy, we can now perceive and welcome them as God's love made visible, made fragrant, made touchable, made audible, made delectable.

Paul put this transformation in summary form when he told his community in Galatia: "I have been crucified with Christ; and it is no longer I who live, but it is Christ who lives in me. And the life I now live in the flesh I live by faith in the Son of God, who loved me and gave himself for me" (Gal. 2:19–20). Saying that Christ lives in him is another way of saying that the animating spirit that shapes his heart and directs his life is now a spirit of "love, joy, peace, patience, kindness, generosity, faithfulness, gentleness, and self-control" (Gal. 5:22–23), all ways of relating that Jesus demonstrated in his own life and now makes possible in us insofar as we are willing to commit ourselves to him. Personal and social healing happen when the "fruit of the Spirit" takes hold in us, when the exercise of love, joy, peace, and kindness turns us toward each other, so that we can be a welcoming and nurturing presence. Baptism is the prerequisite that enables individuals to give themselves to a community that gives itself to the well-being of others.

God's power to re-create human lives is astounding. The Acts of the Apostles records that when the Holy Spirit descended on Christ's followers on the day of Pentecost—in a rush of overpowering wind and animating air—they began to speak in languages not their own (2:4). To share a language is an indispensable element in the sharing of life. If I do not know what you are saying, I am unable to know your need and potential. That these early Christians could suddenly speak another's language indicated that they were ready and empowered to receive and nurture people they did not already know. It showed that they were open to welcome strangers and foreigners, share life with them, and show hospitality. Filled with the Holy Spirit—filled with the love that has circulated through creation from the beginning, the very love that Jesus showed in his ministries of feeding, healing, exorcising, and reconciling others—these disciples could now make their way into a life "full of gladness" (2:28).

This way of gladness led into a deep sharing of life together. Acts records: "All who believed were together and had all things in common; they would sell their possessions and goods and distribute the proceeds to all, as any had need. Day by day, as they spent much time together in the temple, they broke bread at home and ate their food with glad and generous hearts, praising God and having the goodwill of all the people" (2:44–47). So attuned were these people to each other's needs that we are told, "There was not a needy person among them" (4:34)

It is impossible to know how many and to what degree these early Christians practiced the love that Jesus desired for them. What is clear is that the biblical writer understood that the life of sharing is the logical and necessary outcome of people inspired by the Spirit. When the love of Jesus works its way in the world, people become empowered to give themselves to each other in acts of service and mutual nurture. Needs are met, and people are glad.

It should not surprise us that a meal was at the center of this sharing, healing activity. Food is never simply a commodity or fuel that keeps us going on our way. Food is the most basic form of nurture we know. It is the means of life. Grown and shared in a thoughtful manner, it can be the expression of the love that God shows in creating a world that is refreshing, delectable, and enlivening. Every time we prepare a meal, we have the opportunity to communicate how much we love others, how much we want them to enjoy themselves and this world, and how much we want them to thrive in it. Food is an invitation to conviviality, and eating is the enactment of fellowship.

But it can also be an occasion for division. As is well known, eating has often been the most practical way to keep people apart. Tables can be closed to strangers or to people of different ethnic or racial heritage. Dietary rules and prohibitions can be an effective means of segregating who is "in" and who is "out" of a group. This is why early Christians had to learn to eat with everyone. To be unwilling to eat with others is to be unwilling to share life with them. In this unwillingness we see a refusal to share Jesus's healing and nurturing presence in the world.

One of the first to have to learn this lesson was the disciple Peter. As a Jewish Christian, Peter believed it important to maintain the dietary codes that had served Jews for centuries. But as long as Peter maintained these traditions, he would have been prevented from fully sharing in the lives of non-Jews. So God gave Peter a vision in which a large sheet came down from heaven. On this sheet were all kinds of animals, including the animals considered unclean by Jews. Peter then heard a voice telling him to kill and eat. Peter did not want to eat what was unclean and prohibited, so the voice said, "What God has made clean, you must not call profane" (Acts 10:15). Peter had trouble taking this message in—indicating how hard it can be to change our habits—so the vision and message had to be repeated three times!

This is the message: food should not be an excuse to keep people apart. It should, rather, be the occasion that draws us more intimately into each other's lives, so that we can share the pain and possibility, lament the failure, and celebrate the success. To help make this happen, Christians were instructed to eat "in remembrance of Jesus." They were to make their daily meals an occasion in which the love that Jesus showed in his ministries of healing, feeding, exorcising, and reconciling could be extended to the world. They were to eat Jesus as the "bread of life" (John 6:35), who, by entering into their bodies as food, transformed them from within, so that they could become food for those who needed the nurture they could provide. To "remember" Jesus while eating is not to recall a historical curiosity. It is to invite the creative source of life to join our table and heal the relationships happening there. It is to ask God to empower each life, so that it can better meet the needs of others.

It is an odd thing to say Jesus has become your food, perhaps even a bit repulsive if you say you are eating his flesh and drinking his blood (John 6:53). Clearly, Jesus is not asking people to become cannibals! It is important to remember that in the time of Jesus, blood was understood to be the power of life in a living being. To drink Jesus's blood is, therefore, a way of communicating that you want the life force at work in you to be the same life force that was at work in Jesus. To drink Jesus is to take within yourself a fresh, life-giving power. This is why the cup of wine or juice that is offered at a Eucharist is called the "cup of salvation." Similarly with Jesus's flesh. To consume his flesh as the "bread of life" is to invite Jesus into your being in the most intimate way we know: by eating. But unlike normal bread, which disappears by being digested, Jesus remains within us, transforming and empowering us to live the ministering life that he makes possible.

At the Eucharist a kind of marriage happens: we become one flesh with him and commit to live in fidelity to his way of being in the world. Here we receive Jesus as our food, so that we, in turn, can become food for others, nurturing them into the ways of life abundant.

The Eucharist, or Lord's Supper, is so important to the formation of Christian community, because it is in the act of eating that we regularly have the chance to draw close to each other and the creatures that feed us. It is where we take the time to face each other and listen to each other's struggles and triumphs. Communal life requires that people know what is going on in each other's lives. How else will we discover when and how to be a help to each other? How else will we know what or who needs celebrating?

The Eucharist is the meal where we gather with each other around a table, so as to invite the love of God to enter into our stomachs and hearts and from there empower our bodies to live as Jesus did. Here people receive the nurture they need to put the love they have received to work in the world. At the Eucharist we see that the kitchen or dining table takes the place of the classroom desk where we do our exercises in the learning of love.

CHAPTER 12

Love Creates a New World

Love has made me an inventor.
MARGUERITE BARANKITSE ("MAGGY")

THERE IS MORE THAN enough pain and suffering in this world to make us want to give up on love. History is punctuated with the brutality that people regularly inflict on each other. In the twentieth century alone, the century when humanity was supposedly at its most educated, moral best, tens of millions of people (estimates vary between 150 and 200 million) were slaughtered in warfare and various campaigns of starvation, displacement, genocide, terrorism, and torture. Add to that the regular slights, abandonments, and abuses that don't make it in the history books or news, and it is understandable that some will balk at the notion that love can change the world. Love is a good idea, and it's nice when it happens in limited contexts from time to time, but we shouldn't expect it to have much impact in a violent world.

Clearly, love is a vulnerable power. It does not coerce. It does not make its way by violent force. Instead, it receives and absorbs the anger and hate that swirls around it. The cross of Christ is the definitive expression of that. Rather than fleeing the violence that came his way or countering it with yet more violent force, Jesus took it within himself and suffered unto death. The cross is a mirror that compels us to see the full depravity of our being, because it confronts us with the fact that too often we would rather murder love than receive it.

Given the violent and disease-ridden contexts of our world, it is clear that we need examples that teach us how love works to bring about redemption. We need teachers who appreciate the logic of love and know how to apply it in ways that effect healing, reconciliation, and peace. In this chapter I present the story of Maggy, one of the most inspiring contemporary teachers of the love of God I have ever met. In her work in Burundi and in the institutions she has created at Maison Shalom ("House of Peace"), she has shown how love's healing power can take root in some of the most brutal places on earth. In her story many of the themes of Part IV come together in a synthetic and organic way. In her life and witness we have the opportunity to see that people are never condemned to a world bent on destruction and death. When love goes to work, a new world governed by joy and peace and resulting in beauty and mutual flourishing becomes possible.

Meeting Maggy

ON SUNDAY, OCTOBER 24, 1993, Marguerite "Maggy" Barankitse, a Burundian Tutsi, looked out from the bishop's compound to see

Tutsi rebels advancing with clubs, rocks, and machetes. The newly elected Hutu president, Melchior Ndadaye, had recently been assassinated by Tutsis. As a retaliatory measure, Hutus took to the streets on a rampage, killing any Tutsis who could be found. Tutsis countered with violent vengeance of their own. Burundi was being turned once again into a vast killing field, as families that had once been friends now turned savagely against each other.

Among the rebels approaching the bishop's compound that day, Maggy spotted several of her Tutsi cousins and neighbors. After hiding the children in her care, Maggy confronted them: "Why are you here? You are Christians. These are your brothers. You deny your baptism by your violence." Her plea had no effect. The rebels poured gasoline on the building where they suspected Maggy's Hutu friends were hiding. They then ordered whoever was inside to come out or risk being burned alive. Dozens of screaming Hutu women and children fled the building as many more attackers waited for them outside. No one escaped.

Though Maggy had given money to the rebels in hopes of saving the children, the men stripped her naked, tied her to a chair, and then made her watch as they proceeded to slaughter seventy-two people right before her eyes. The sounds of machetes hacking and children screaming filled the morning air. Among the victims was her best friend, Juliette, the mother of two young girls. Days before, perhaps sensing that violence would engulf her and her doctor husband, Cyprien, Juliette had asked Maggy to take care of her young daughters, Lydia and Lysette. Now about to be butchered, Juliette said, "You will raise our babies. They won't kill you." In the presence of both girls, the rebels cut off Juliette's head and threw it in Maggy's lap. Fire, chaos, and bloodshed were everywhere. Sitting in the chair, Maggy could think of nothing to do except pray for the killers.

When the massacre ended, Maggy was released by a rebel named Edward, who said, "Now, Maggy, your Hutu friends await you."

What she encountered was a compound strewn with limbs, heads, and mutilated corpses. The ground was red with blood. She went to the charred chapel in anguish, hoping to find survivors. Outside the chapel she found a small body whose smashed head moved slightly. There was no face to recognize, only blood, skin, and lips that had been beaten into a grotesque shape. She gently picked up and held the child close. Trembling, she continued on, looking for more survivors. Maggy longed for night, so she would not have to see so clearly.

Though she had no biological children of her own, all Maggy could think of was saving as many kids as she could. Recalling the events of that day, Maggy says, "It was the needs of those children that drove and inspired me. I had these children in the beginning, and I had nothing to offer them. They needed love, they needed safety, and they needed food and clothing. I simply had to invent ways to help them."[1]

Years earlier Maggy had been a schoolteacher, but then lost her job because she protested the discriminatory education policies and practices aimed at Hutus. She left for a time to study in Switzerland, but then returned to become a secretary to the bishop. Soon after, she began adopting Hutu and Tutsi children, believing that the future of Burundi depended on mutual understanding and peace. She had brought these children to the bishop's compound for safety as the situation in Burundi became increasingly violent. Miraculously, all seven of Maggy's adopted kids, along with several more for a total of twenty-five, survived the October massacre.

The violence of 1993 was not new to Maggy or the people of Burundi. In the three previous decades, massacres of Hutus and Tutsis occurred in 1965, 1972, 1988, and 1991. Maggy was sick and tired of it. It was as if a collective amnesia had settled over the country; everyone looked away and refused to acknowledge or address the slaughter of family members and all the orphans it was creating. No one talked about the hatred. No one committing the bloodshed was brought to justice. Hope for forgiveness and reconciliation, and with it the prospect of a peaceful life together, seemed to be in no one's heart or imagination. And so hatred festered, and the fires of revenge smoldered. It was as if people had given up on love, or at least given up on love as a power that can guide communities, tribes, even the nation as a whole.

It would be too easy to think that Burundi had suddenly been taken over by evil monsters and that all traces of compassion had simply left the land. It is naive and unrealistic to expect fallible people to show love in its unadulterated purity. We need to remember that among the rebels storming the compound were husbands, sons, fathers, and friends who, in other circumstances, likely "loved" their significant others. But something had gone terribly wrong. Their hearts had become sick. Perhaps their imaginations had become so degraded that the thought of killing a stranger was not only possible, but necessary. Perhaps their affections and sympathies were so narrowed as to render their love in other areas suspect. Or perhaps they were simply weak or cowards and did not have the courage to resist mob hysteria. If we "love" only the people it is convenient or useful to love or if love excuses violent action to protect or enhance it, is it really love?

The massacres of 1993 were but one more result of a country's diseased imagination, the sort of imagination that limits and distorts love's work by placing fear and hatred at the core of human hearts. Once a heart is made sick by violence, it is hard to heal. How are the hundreds of thousands of children made permanently afraid by seeing their mothers and fathers, their sisters and brothers beaten, raped, and murdered to learn to trust and love? How are the citizens of Burundi, a fertile land rich with productive potential, to be expected to commit to rebuilding their nation when its children are being denied the hope of a safe and meaningful life? One of the great tragedies, in Maggy's eyes, was that these children were being deprived of a future by being deprived of the daily love that makes people want a future. They were being raised to believe that violence is normal and that hatred and fear can coexist with love.

Maggy had once thought of fleeing the madness and returning to Switzerland, but now, looking at the face of the mutilated child in her arms, she realized that she could never leave. She had to gather the children and bury the dead. Maggy says the resolve to go on came to her as an unanticipated gift: "I felt this incredible resistance inside me, like strength. . . . As soon as I knew that my children had survived, I felt a strong will to live. I could think of one thing and only one thing: taking care of them, raising them beyond this hatred and bitterness that I came to see in their eyes."[2]

The way ahead would not be easy. Maggy gathered the surviving children, washed their wounds, and tried to comfort them. As darkness approached, she shepherded them to a neighbor's house, making sure that none of them got swept up in the sea of thousands fleeing the region for Tanzania. Refugees were everywhere. Along the way, Maggy faced the taunts of neighboring women who derided her as a traitor for taking in Hutu children. When she finally reached the house, she found that several nuns and priests were already there. Close to seventy people slept behind the walls of that home. The work of burying the dead and finding food and clothing consumed Maggy in the days that followed. Though she would later collapse from exhaustion and the buildup of trauma, now was not the time to cry. Maggy knew she had to smile and be enthusiastic, because without her positive spirit the children would not be able to go on. She had to inspire in these children a desire to sing and dance again.

Having witnessed so much suffering and bloodshed on that brutal October day, Maggy looked to the children to determine what needed to be done—need being a perpetual invitation to love to come and go to work—so that the people of Burundi could have a future worth living for. She knew that such a future depended on forgiveness and reconciliation, because without them there could be no true peace. She knew that it depended on children living safely in their own homes, having a strong sense of human dignity and personal freedom, and being surrounded by family and people who loved them. She knew that getting there was going to be hard.

Just how hard became clear in the appearance of nine-year-old Justine. Justine came to Maggy not long after the massacre when a neighbor killed her parents and her sister. Maggy resolved to go back to Justine's village to rebuild her parents' house. Justine, however, insisted that they call on the man who had killed her family to show him the burned remains of the house and make an offer of reconciliation. Maggy was surprised, but Justine said that the house could not be rebuilt without first rebuilding the heart that had been destroyed in the violence. She said, "I want to *live*. . . . If I hate him, I can't live. . . . The hatred stops me from continuing to live."

Maggy accompanied Justine on her journey to her family's killer. Justine said to the man, "I want to ask you to ask me for forgiveness. I am able to forgive you." The man was shocked by the child's request. He was even more astounded by her request that he become her father: "Because you can't give me back my father, my mom, my sister, I ask you to become my father." The man accepted, and they rebuilt the house together. When he became ill several years later, Justine took care of him. At his funeral she cried and brought flowers for him. Shortly before his death, he said to Maggy, "Thank you, Maggy. Because now I am dying like a human person, not like a killer. Your forgiveness gave me back hope, love, life."[3]

Learning from Maggy

As a child Maggy was much influenced by her Christian mother, Thérèse, who practiced the radical love of Jesus: she was cheerful, kind, and extremely generous with those who had need. On her way to Mass she often took food with her to the local hospital, offering it to anyone who did not have enough to eat. When Thérèse saw street children alone, she would bring them to her house, feed them lunch, and then invite them to dance on the lawn outside. Above all, Thérèse wanted people to know that God created humanity to enjoy life and welcome it as a gift.

Maggy grew up wanting to live this gospel, this "good news" life too, because she was attracted to love's inherent goodness and beauty. Early on she knew that God's love, the kind of love that welcomed and empowered everyone, forbade the kind of ethnic hatred and violence that was destroying her country. Love cannot willfully exclude anyone because, as she read in her Bible, "Love is patient; love is kind; love is not envious or boastful or arrogant or rude. It does not insist on its own way; it is not irritable or resentful; it does not rejoice in wrongdoing, but rejoices in the truth. It bears all things, believes all things, hopes all things, endures all things" (1 Cor. 13:4–7).

To meet Maggy is to meet kindness. It is to meet a person who is ready to welcome everyone and is willing to walk through life's joys and pains with them. This hardly makes Maggy a pushover: she has talked down men who came to assassinate her and then employed them in her work at her communal compound called Maison Shalom, the "home of peace"! As Maggy sees it, to wrong another human being is an offense of the highest order, because in such wrongdoing the gift of God that another person is has been denied. Love has made Maggy the champion of all people, especially children, which is why she had to protest discriminatory practices in the schools.

Maggy was seeing that without God's love the children of Burundi would be without peace and without hope. Love drives out fear and frees people to enter more fully into life with others. Fear and hatred, however, destroy the heart, causing people to grab and degrade life rather than nurture it. They destroy human sympathy and imagination, making it impossible for people to live with others with joy. This is why Maggy likes to say, "Our human vocation is to love. I was created out of love, to love. This is the most beautiful calling of the human being. God created us to be happy. We need to be able to sing and dance. When we can't sing anymore, then life has gone out of us." Love is so vital and so necessary, because it is our best attempt to affirm the goodness and beauty of what is.

But love is not easy, especially in a place like Burundi, where a spirit of suspicion, resentment, and vengeance had come to rule. How can anyone welcome, let alone dance with, killers? How can murderers like Justine's "father" be embraced as fellow children of God and then invited to make a new family? Maggy had seen that Christians easily forget or deny the love of Jesus and then practice a corrupt and bankrupt form of Christianity. She witnessed Christianity's corruption in self-professing Christians who said they were Hutus or Tutsis first and then proceeded to torture and kill the other group. She saw it in Christians who thought nothing of burning and looting church grounds and slaughtering fellow Christians. What these people failed to realize is that love and violence are incompatible, because violence is an assault on the life that love affirms and seeks to nurture.

Maggy realized that Christians are as susceptible to sin as anyone else. Faced with injustice and horror or caught in the grip of fear, they want to judge, punish, and exact revenge. But in failing to love as Jesus loved, they also forfeit life. "When we forgive, we give life to others, but also to ourselves. Because the person who doesn't forgive does not exist. You know, when you refuse to forgive, you stop living."[4] Forgiveness is crucial because it lifts the weight of guilt, remorse, and debt. It liberates people to make a fresh start in life, no longer tied down by the chains of past wrongdoing.

What Maggy saw is that *people can exist, but fail to live.* When they fail to live, it is *because they fail to love.* People are created to experience the rich life of communion, a life in which they learn to be sources of help and joy to each other. To turn against another, whether in small acts of antagonism or brutal acts of violence, is to forget that life can only fully become itself or reach its full potential when it is enjoyed *together*.

For Maggy, the love of Jesus changes everything. It opens a world of possibility that includes peace, hope, and the prospect of a joyful life together. Maggy likes to say, "Love has made me an inventor." What she means is that love creates a new imagination, enabling people to see needs and possibilities for flourishing that others cannot. Burundi had become a killing field that produces orphans, but this did not confine or limit her imagination.

Inspired by the love of God, Maggy has committed all her energies to building a community that would eventually enable her to take care of tens of thousands of children. Over several years Maggy has constructed over three thousand homes, a cinema and hotel and restaurant, education facilities, multiple farm fields, and a hospital, which all together go by the name of Maison Shalom. She has encouraged microfinance, developed employment programs, and built an extensive physical infrastructure to take care of Burundi's many problems. It is the sort of imagination that, for instance, prompted her to build a swimming pool in the very place that was once a killing field. Love is stronger than hatred and violence, and the proof of that is that children can now splash and laugh and play where once children were put to death.

What love does is create the desire and inspire the practical skill to assist others. Maggy says, "If you love, you will find new ways to give." In the giving of themselves to others, people discover, often in ways that they could not have anticipated, that they can now do what they could not do before. In numerous interviews Maggy has stated that her work would not be possible without the help of others, especially the children. They give her encouragement. They give her ideas. They show her a path forward when she thinks she is lost. To help others she has to be willing to be helped herself. The intervention of a kind word or act always has the potential to radically alter the course of the life it meets. Imagine a world in which the people you meet are not threats or competitors, but agents devoted to your well-being and joy. That would be a world inspired by love.

Maggy was inspired and empowered to do the work she was doing because she believed that Jesus's self-offering love creates genuine life, the kind of life that has moved beyond the diminished sort of existence governed by loneliness, anxiety, and violence. It is the love of God that creates community, what Christians sometimes call the family of God, made up of countless sisters and brothers. It is the love of God that inspires the will to build something so outrageous as a movie theater, so that children of war can imagine a different world. It is the Christian declaration that all people are God's children that renders void the tribal claim that one is first a Hutu or a Tutsi. It is God's love that helps people know that victims *and* the perpetrators of violence need healing and their sense of dignity restored. It is the love of God that opens a future worth striving for.

Maggy believes that the day love disappears entirely from life is also the day a worthwhile world disappears:

> If I were not a Christian, I would have committed suicide many times over the years. It is my faith that gives me strength. Whenever I face difficulties, I go to church and pray to God to remove the obstacles that are in my path. And God answers my prayers. It is my faith that gives me the peace and confidence to hope in the darkest moments for a spirit of love that will allow us to forgive and to be reconciled.[5]

Faith, however, is not a simple or automatic thing. Though it is an act of trust in God, it is also mixed with doubt and anger. Maggy recalls that, after the horror of the 1993 massacre and her own family's involvement in it, she went into the chapel and cried, "Oh God, my mom lied to me, because she taught me that you are love. How you can create how I belong to those killers? I don't believe that you are love." Having witnessed such horror and being in the grip of fear and an overwhelming sense of futility, Maggy did not know that she could trust God or if God was even worthy of trust. What kept her going was the voice of her first adoptive child, Chloe, who reassured her that God's commitment to life is not a lie. The sign of that was the fact that they were still alive and that God wanted to work through them to bring healing into the world.

Another difficult time for Maggy occurred in 1996. Having traveled to Butezi, the site of yet another massacre, Maggy encountered the mutilated bodies of more mothers and children. The stress of months of exhausting work and the trauma of having witnessed so much brutality came together, causing Maggy to collapse. Tears streamed down her face. Maggy was unable to speak for a month. A doctor informed her that she was suffering from total exhaustion.

During this time a Carmelite convent sheltered Maggy and gave her the room to face the pain and shame of all the brutality she had witnessed. She struggled mightily with the questions: Why bother to love when there is so much hatred everywhere? Is it not cruel to love children only to release them into a violent world that makes a mockery of this love? Maggy was angry with herself for thinking that she should or could help the children. She was angry with God. But prayer helped her find her way then, as it still does today. She needed to pray so that she could come to a time of self-examination and listening for God, a place of honesty about herself and what she needed to do.

Maggy gradually understood that the work of healing is not hers, but God's. "It's not me; it's the hand of God. I am a little instrument." And so she prayed, "Give me enough strength to go and to bright Your glory, not me, but You." Maggy came to see that it is not her responsibility to remake people or change the world into the image she has chosen. She is but a participant in God's love, allowing God's love to flow through her. Maggy realized that she could only return to health if she humbly relied on God and others. Rather than being the boss, Maggy would need to become a servant enabling others to become the creatures God had made them to be. She needed to learn that God is at the center and the source of whatever strength she had. She needed the Eucharist to feed her to do God's work. Her daily prayer became: "Let me not become an obstacle to the miracles You will perform today."

It was the realization that her life was intimately connected to God's love at work in the world that enabled Maggy to begin her true life's work. Sometimes she compares Maison Shalom to a large ship. God is the captain. She is one of the crew running the ship, so that it can reach the destination where all people are one family of love:

> Before it was me, Maggy, that helped a few people; but in 1993, after such great pain, I felt the call to leave it all behind and count on God's mighty power. I devoted myself entirely to their service. I was driven by this inexplicable strength; I had not eaten anything in two days, but I wasn't the least bit hungry. I had plenty of energy. I had never felt closer to God than on that day. I was completely helpless, but strengthened by love. I was exhausted, but there wasn't the slightest bit of despair on my face.[6]

No longer despondent or afraid—death threats would become a common occurrence—Maggy set to work. Her task is not to "save" the world or even all the children of Burundi. It is to bear witness to the love of God. If the love of God is forgotten, the noble intentions

of people to save others will become destructive, because the desire
for power will overrun the desire to help:

> Even though I was so busy, I know my first mission is not to
> take care of the children. It's to announce the gospel . . . to
> announce the good news. . . . This message doesn't belong to
> me. It's my vocation. . . . I want to tell to all those people that
> evil will never take the last word. It's always the love.[7]

PART V

Hope

CHAPTER 13

When Love Is All in All,
Life Is Heaven

So if anyone is in Christ, there is a new creation: everything old
has passed away; see, everything has become new!
2 CORINTHIANS 5:17

HEAVEN IS THE GOAL and fulfillment of the Christian drama, because heaven marks the time when love is "all in all." As the previous chapters have shown, from a Christian point of view, love is the power that brings creatures into existence and daily sustains them in their being. But as we all know, creatures live in a world of wounds. Love has become corrupted, and life has been damaged as a result. The love of God, however, never gives up on creatures. It sets to work to bring about the healing of wounds. Insofar as healing is received in this life, however provisionally, people experience a taste of heaven. When the healing is complete, when no creature is in pain, and when injustice is no more, then the fullness of heaven will have arrived. Heaven is the time when everything that moves moves only under the power of the love of God. It is the time when every relationship is governed by nurture, flourishing, and celebration.

The hope of heaven, the subject of the last part of this book, is the ultimate purpose and goal of the drama of love. Love is complete when love alone is the power that moves through life. In this time and place creatures no longer face any threatening or debilitating power. They meet nothing that means to do them harm or injury, because love has overcome all the powers of degradation and evil. Clearly, we are not there yet. Nor do we know exactly or comprehensively what the life of heaven will be, since our imaginations are currently too small and our hearts too impure. Even so, heaven's full realization is something we yearn for as love's fulfillment and promise. Christian hope rests in the ultimate victory of love over hate, a victory that is signaled in Jesus's own overcoming of violence and death with his resurrection from the dead on Easter.

It is easy to be confused about hope, especially when we take into account that many of us have hearts that are hurting or sick. Misconceptions about heaven abound. In this chapter we begin by clarifying some of the basics about heaven, so that in the next chapter we can start to appreciate the harmonious character of heavenly life.

Heaven is both an indispensable and a dangerous idea. It is indispensable, because it gives us a vision through which the realities of this life can be evaluated and improved. If heaven represents the complete realization of life as it is meant to be—of life in its just, healed, and perfected state—then it cannot only matter for some future time. Appreciating the hope it communicates and glimpsing some of its practical features enable people to correct the wrongs of life as they are currently experienced. The Lord's Prayer asks that God's will and way of ordering life be realized here, "on earth as it is in heaven" (Matt. 6:10), indicating that heaven is to be tasted and savored even now. Heaven and hope go together, because heaven is the assurance that God does not abandon the world, but is committed to healing all its wounds. Heaven is forever desirable, because it is the place and time in which the love of God is fully and freely at work in all creatures.

The Dangers of Heaven

HEAVEN IS A SUPREMELY dangerous idea, for two primary reasons. First, it can serve as a conceptual club that divides people into the damned and the saved, and then condemns the damned into hell. Invariably (and conveniently), the one wielding the club is among the saved. And, second, it can function as an idea that promotes *escape* from the hard realities of this life, as when people say it is best to endure meekly and quietly the injustices of this life, because it will all be better somewhere else after we die. Both positions represent a rejection of the logic of love: the former by venting hatred toward others and the latter by failing to put love to work in the world.

The first of the dangers became especially clear to me several years ago when my family and I lived in Saskatoon, Canada. I had taken a two-year teaching position at St. Thomas More College at the University of Saskatchewan. We loved this city and the neighborhood in which we lived. The work was good, and we were becoming friends with some very special people. We were even a bit hesitant to leave for summer vacation after the first year.

The trouble began when we returned from our trip. The owner of the house we rented came for a visit and told us we were being evicted. He was quitting his out-of-town job early and wanted to live in his own house. I told him that his wife promised we could stay in the house the full two years (she clearly thought they wouldn't return home within that time). He wasn't interested in what his wife had said. He saw no reason why he should look for a rental property when he owned the house we were living in. He planned to move in. We were out.

I was furious. Classes were about to start, and I had a lot of work to do to prepare for the fall semester. I didn't have the time to pack up a house, nor did my wife. She had her hands full with our two very young daughters. Besides, all the good rental houses had been snapped up by others who made their plans months before. Moving is a huge emotional and practical ordeal, even in the best of circumstances. How would we manage it all?

During the ensuing days the injustice of our predicament festered in my mind. I was angry with myself for taking the man and his wife at their word and not having secured a written contract specifying that the rental was for two years. I quickly demonized the husband as evil incarnate and longed for justice, or at least some small opening for revenge. Perhaps I should give the girls brushes and wild colors with which to paint the house? But I couldn't exact my own revenge, because I knew that I would likely need to list him as a reference when, sometime later, I would apply for a mortgage (I imagined the colorful letter he would provide if we wrecked his house!). When I saw that there was little I could do against him, my mind went cosmic and eternal. Justice, as I saw it, would not be done here and now, but he would get his rightful punishment in the next life. God was on my side, and God would punish this wicked man, sending him straight to hell! I, meanwhile, would have a front-row seat in heaven, where I could watch his torments.

Looking back, I now find my sentiment almost laughable, were it not so hateful. That I wished this man to experience the torments of hell was a sign that I possessed a sick heart. But the sickness is hardly unique to me. There is significant psychological pleasure in being able to characterize oneself as a victim of injustice and then, like a god, be able to consign the agents of wrongdoing to a hell designed especially for them. It makes the hurt and suffering feel less painful somehow. As the innocent being wronged, I could convince myself not only that God is on my side, but that God will make sure I enter the gates of heaven. There I will experience all the joys that were unjustly denied me in my present life, including the joy of seeing the people who wronged me get their just punishment.

The German philosopher Friedrich Nietzsche saw in this psychological mechanism a reflection of a resentful and spiteful heart. The mechanism works like this. Individuals, communities, and even whole nations dearly want life to go in ways that contribute to their own flourishing. When things don't go as planned or desired, they want to find someone to blame: Jews, women, white trash, white privilege, blacks, Arabs, conservatives, liberals, Muslims, homosexuals, heterosexuals, the 1 percent, illegal immigrants, legal immigrants, bosses, workers . . . Everyone and anyone can be at fault. People want to establish the moral order that puts them in the right and others in the wrong. The result, however, is a vision of heaven and hell that is the psychological *projection* of people who are expressing their frustration and hatred in this life. It is a vision that then underwrites all kinds of social hierarchies establishing who is "in" and who is "out." With walls and hierarchies in place, people now have the excuse they need to love selectively, if they love at all. Heaven is the place where people are just like me, sharing the same aspirations and rewards as me. Hell is its mirror opposite.

John Lennon was right to criticize this idea of heaven. In the song "Imagine," one of the most performed and historically significant songs of the twentieth century (*Rolling Stone* magazine put it at number 3 on its list of "The 500 Greatest Songs of All Time"), he asked his listeners to envision and then create a world without heaven and hell, a world without the divisions that religions, nationalities, and possessions can inspire. In his view, the idea of heaven needs to be dropped, because it is too often used to damn and exclude people. What Lennon sought was a world in which people came together in peace. People would live for the moment, no longer driven by absolutes or by greed. The reasons to kill others would have disappeared. People would share what they have and form one vast family living in unity and equality.

Lennon's sentiment, though sometimes criticized as naive, even hypocritical—did he, a millionaire, really expect people to live without possessions?—has clearly struck a chord. "Imagine" is still regularly performed and listened to around the world. In some countries, it functions like a national anthem, and on some occasions it plays the role of an international call to peace, as when it closed the 2012 Olympics.

But what if the Christian understanding of heaven was never meant to function in the exclusionary, judgmental, damning ways that Lennon supposes? And what if a characterization of heaven as *the love of God becoming fully active in the lives of all creatures* turns out to be a better and more realistic teaching for moving the world toward peace and joy? This is a possibility that the song "Imagine" does not imagine.

Let's look now at the other danger of heaven—when it functions as an escape from the troubles of this life. Think of the numbers of people through the ages who have been told that, rather than work to change circumstances of injustice, it is best to accept the pain coming their way and wait patiently for the time when they will enjoy their reward in heaven. Heaven is seen as having nothing to do with the events of this world, because it has been thoroughly spiritualized, turned into a soft and cushy place for individuals' souls. It is an ethereal place that welcomes the wounded and downtrodden only after they die. This "pie in the sky" heaven is portrayed as the ultimate *release* from all the suffering of embodiment and all the tension of our entanglement with others. It is the place where individuals get to enjoy all the things they were deprived of in this life.

The central problem with this characterization of heaven is that it simply sweeps aside the ambiguity and hurt of this life and thus demonstrates that it does not take seriously the beauty, difficulty, and complexity of our embodied life together. Body-soul dualism resides deep within this vision: bodies don't really matter, but ethereal souls do. That means the world of bodies, which is to say the whole of this created world, will ultimately be left behind. When heaven is presented as an escape from this world, it is clear that this world was never truly appreciated as the place where God's love is made material. Because all the emphasis is on anticipating all the good that will come *after* people die, people are freed of the need to love and accept responsibility for the world *before* they die. Heaven as *escape* from the world amounts to an *evasion,* even an *abandonment* of life, which is why this characterization of heaven is a theological disaster.

As we will see, the desire to escape is understandable. People prefer to look *up* and *away,* because to look *down* and *around* is to see the mess that we have made of our world and our lives. It is to face and have to deal with all the pain and needless suffering we have introduced into the world. Rather than stay and work to improve things, however, people sing of the desire to "fly away." The sentiment I am describing can be clearly seen in the lyrics of the popular gospel song "This World Is Not My Home," written by J. R. Baxter Jr.:

> *This world is not my home, I'm just a-passing through.*
> *My treasures are laid up, somewhere beyond the blue.*
> *The angels beckon me from heaven's open door,*
> *And I can't feel at home in this world anymore.*[1]

When people believe the world is not their home, it is much less likely that they will love it deeply and learn to care for it properly. It will function like a motel: something to be used more or less thoughtlessly, but not to be appreciated in its own right.

When religion is presented as the means whereby people get to an otherworldly heaven, it is deserving of the critique made famous by Karl Marx. Marx called religion the opium of people, because heaven functions as the excuse not to deal with the hatred, wounds, and injustices that are most often the effects of human decision and action. He wanted people to work for their real happiness rather than pine for an illusory happiness that is promised them after they die. But to do that, they needed to return their attention to this world and get busy changing the social and economic structures that keep them deprived of the good that could be theirs.

Heaven on Earth

WHAT IF A CHRISTIAN understanding of heaven is not about escaping the world's pain and trouble, but is instead about receiving, sharing, and extending the love of God every place we find ourselves in? And what if faith's movement is not to take us out of the world but, following God's own lead in the life of Jesus, to learn to be *with* creatures in all their struggles and joys?

Christianity is genuinely "good news" insofar as it proclaims that *in the person of Jesus Christ the life of heaven has come to earth*. Not an idea about heaven, but heaven itself, in the flesh. The incarnation of God in Jesus is the definitive expression of the divine desire that God's eternal life of love be made real in this temporal world. God creates, so that each creature can share in the joy and delight that is God's own life. This assumes that no creature is wasted, left behind, or forgotten. All are only loved—loved forever. The logic of God's love is such that it seeks to become fully active in everything.

This is an astounding claim to make. The life of this world may be punctuated by all kinds of diminishment, pain, and injustice, but the presence of Jesus in the world changes everything: loneli-

ness is met with companionship, fear is turned into hope, violation
is overcome by love, and sadness is turned to joy. Jesus is the light
enabling people to journey out of their darkness. He is the salt that
makes life's nurture delectable. In him the wounds of this world and
this life are taken up and healed. Jesus wants people to know life at
its best. He wants them to see it, touch it, smell it, hear it, and taste
it *right now.*

To read the Bible is to see that from beginning to end God is
Emmanuel, "God with us." God does not ever flee from creation.
Instead, God is continually moving toward it, becoming more intimate with it, because intimacy is the goal of love. In an image
that should shock us, scripture ends with God—and therefore also
the life of heaven—descending to earth, because "the home of
God is among mortals. He will dwell with them; they will be his
peoples, and God himself will be with them" (Rev. 21:3). All the
souls that have been yearning to flee to an otherworldly heaven
will surely be shocked when they discover that God is moving in
the opposite direction. Heaven is not found by *ascending* to some
faraway place, but by the love of God *descending* into the lives of
creatures.

Heaven is the time and place in which creatures experience life
fully transformed by love. That means Christians should stop looking for (or fighting over!) the ticket that will give them entrance to
the super theme park called "Heaven." The problem with the ticket
idea is that it puts all the emphasis on the location: when we get to
heaven everything is going to be so wonderful. But why should
we think that? Creation was first made by God as a paradise. What
makes us think that, entering a heavenly theme park, we will not
damage it just as we have damaged this world? Though heaven is
clearly a place in which the bodies of all creatures experience the
joys of fully realized love, the point is not to look for a special location or some specific quadrant of the universe. The point is to receive and participate in the transformative love that changes us and

our world, so that no matter where we are, life is experienced as the power of nurture and flourishing and celebration. To gain entrance to heaven is not to go somewhere else or to some faraway location, but to be fully healed by love wherever we are, and so experience everything as redeemed and made new.

The transformative movement I am talking about has been captured beautifully in one of Wendell Berry's Sabbath poems:

O saints, if I am eligible for this prayer,
though less than worthy of this dear desire,
and if your prayers have influence in Heaven,
let my place there be lower than your own.
I know how you longed, here where you lived
as exiles, for the presence of the essential
Being and Maker and Knower of all things.
But because of my unruliness, or some erring
virtue in me never rightly schooled,
some error clear and dear, my life
has not taught me your desire for flight:
dismattered, pure, and free. I long
instead for the Heaven of creatures, of seasons,
of day and night. Heaven enough for me
would be this world as I know it, but redeemed
of our abuse of it and one another. It would be
the Heaven of knowing again. There is no marrying
in Heaven, and I submit; even so, I would like
to know my wife again, both of us young again,
and I remembering always how I loved her
when she was old. I would like to know
my children again, all my family, all my dear ones,
to see, to hear, to hold, more carefully
than before, to study them lingeringly as one
studies old verses, committing them to heart

forever. I would like again to know my friends,
my old companions, men and women, horses
and dogs, in all the ages of our lives, here
in this place that I have watched over all my life
in all its moods and seasons, never enough.
I will be leaving how many beauties overlooked?
A painful Heaven this would be, for I would know
by it how far I have fallen short. I have not
paid enough attention, I have not been grateful
enough. And yet this pain would be the measure
of my love. In eternity's once and now, pain would
place me surely in the Heaven of my earthly love.[2]

Heaven Is for Resurrected Bodies

SOMETIMES WHEN I ASK people what it is they are looking forward to in heaven, they have surprisingly little to say. "It's gonna be great!" and "I'm not going to be in pain anymore" are about as specific as it gets. When I ask, "Are we going to eat, play, make art, or make love?" it sounds scandalous. I now think that we have such trouble imagining heaven, because we have made heaven a place exclusively for disembodied souls. Since none of us knows what a disembodied life looks like, we can't really anticipate or work toward heaven. What could we possibly do in heaven if our bodies are dead in the ground?

The idea that heaven is a place for disembodied souls is not a Christian teaching. Christians affirm the "resurrection of the body" rather than the "immortality of the soul," because the soul's immortality represents a rejection of the logic of love, whereas the body's resurrection represents love's strongest affirmation. To be confused about the difference between resurrection and immortality is to fail to understand the radical nature of love's way of life.

The idea that human beings have immortal souls runs deep in ancient thought, but its most influential expression comes from Socrates. Socrates taught that a human being is a duality: a material body and an immaterial soul. Bodies are places of imperfection, suffering, transience, decay, sickness, and death. Though we may relish youthful bodies for their strength, beauty, and endurance, the fact is that everyone's body falls apart and becomes a growing source of misery as it gets old. We only need to visit a nursing facility for the elderly to appreciate how miserable embodied life can become. But even when people are young, they spend a lot of time and resources worrying about whether they look good. Thinking oneself unattractive or ugly is the source of so much personal pain.

Moreover, bodies are the cause of far too much trouble as people seek to fulfill their desires for sex, wealth, power, comfort, or fame. How many women daily undergo the degradations of pornographic desires? How much conflict and how many wars are the result of people seeking to get more for themselves? Will we go so far as to destroy our lands and waters, so that we can enjoy cheap, convenient food? On so many fronts we can see that the quest to satisfy a body's desires is an invitation to turmoil and destruction. Bodies are, in the end, evil.

It isn't that hard, therefore, to appreciate why Socrates taught that we should give no attention or devotion to a body's appetites. Instead, we should focus our minds on philosophical pursuits that train us away from this world and toward an eternal realm of unchanging truth, goodness, and beauty. Death is actually a happy thing, provided one has been a good philosopher, because death is the moment when the soul is finally freed from its wearisome body and released to enter an ethereal realm of spiritual bliss.

Socrates lived his message. While waiting in prison to die, knowing that his death was imminent, he was calmly composing poetry. Though his friends and disciples wept and wailed, he was happy anticipating his future life. Socrates could not wait to leave this material world and its life, because they are only a vale of trouble and tears. The best life couldn't really begin until death freed the soul to live its immortal life. It is little wonder that, facing death calmly as he did, Socrates has been an inspiration to so many people.

Body-soul dualism is a profoundly anti-Christian teaching, because it pronounces evil and despicable what God has made good. No Christian should denounce bodies, because each body is God's love made visible, tactile, audible, fragrant, and nutritious. *Divine love does not ever abandon material reality, because matter is itself the embodiment of love.* Clearly, bodies do become the source of pain and frustration, decay and death, but the response should not be one of Socratic despising and abandonment.

As the life and ministry of Jesus show, the appropriate and most faithful response to a hurt body is to heal it, to a lonely body to touch it, to a hungry body to feed it, to a demon-possessed body to exorcise it and fill it with a life-giving, love-promoting spirit. If Christians were supposed to despise embodiment and all the mess and complication that embodiment necessarily entails, then they would also have to reject the claim that God fully entered into and identified with the physical body of Jesus of Nazareth. But this they cannot do, because as John's gospel famously puts it, Jesus the eternal Word "became flesh and lived among us" (1:14). God does not despise flesh. Instead, God inhabits it so as to heal it from within and lead it into fullness of life.

Jesus's approach to material bodies is the mirror opposite of Socrates's. This is why Jesus does not welcome death (or sickness or hunger or defilement or loneliness). Any power that attacks or degrades bodily life is an attack on the love of God. God's response to the violent attack on a body is not to free the soul from it, leaving the body behind to waste away. Instead, it is to resurrect Christ's tortured and crucified body to new life, the sort of life in which death and degradation no longer have dominating roles, and then to present that new embodied life to the world as the physical evidence and promise of the life it has yet to receive and enjoy.

Material bodies are not incidental to faith, nor are they to be excluded from heaven. They are the medium through which faith is worked out and love is realized. Nothing God has made is beside the point or to be despised. Instead, creatures are to be gratefully received and enjoyed, "For everything created by God is good, and nothing is to be rejected, provided it is received with thanksgiving; for it is sanctified by God's word and by prayer" (1 Tim. 4:4–5). Nothing will be forgotten either, which is why, in the end, all things in heaven and on earth will be gathered up in Christ and then reconciled, so that God's love can be "all in all" (Eph. 1:23; 4:6).

This is another way of saying that the ultimate goal of the whole creation is for every creature to be so suffused and empowered by Jesus's love that its life is an unending witness to the ways of peace and joy. When God's love is "all in all," life is pure enjoyment and delight, because every relationship is one of nurture and care. Try to imagine what life would be like if everything and everyone who touched you sought only your good. That would be something like the life of heaven.

The resurrection of a body is not to be confused with the resuscitation of a corpse (though Jesus's raising of people like Lazarus from the dead is an indication of God's power over death). Resuscitated corpses occupy a realm that is still entirely susceptible to the pain and suffering of the world and thus are an expression of a wounded life. Resuscitated bodies, like Lazarus's, will die again. Resurrected bodies, however, are the material manifestation of a healed body witnessing to a world in which pain and suffering, degradation and violence have come to an end. Resurrected bodies will not die again. They will live forever because mortality has been "swallowed up by life" (2 Cor. 5:4).

Without doubt, to speak of the resurrection of bodies is to speak of a miraculous transformation of life and of bodies, a transformation that is extremely difficult for us to understand. But should this miracle of resurrected life be any more impossible than the miracle of created life? The mechanics of creation and resurrection are simply beyond our intellectual reach. Moreover, the only life we have ever known is one that is saturated with wounds of all kinds, making it really difficult for us to imagine a life in which the wounding of each other has come to an end. This is why we have to be careful not to presume too much in our thinking and descriptions of heaven: our love is too small and too imperfect to ascertain, let alone comprehend, the depth and transformative power of God's love.

What does a world entirely saturated and animated by God's love look like? The best that we can do is try to glimpse and gain a taste of what is yet to be by considering what the life of Jesus teaches. The key is to welcome Christ's love to heal and animate our own, because it is then that our eyes are gradually opened to the resurrected life that is possible.

None of us know the mechanics of resurrection or the precise nature of a resurrected body. What we have to guide us is the reality of Jesus's resurrected body, a body that ate and bore the healed scars of hatred, a body that could be touched, but also a body that mysteriously entered rooms that were locked. When Paul tried to make sense of a resurrected body, he concluded that it is a "spiritual body" (Gk. *soma pneumatikon*), indicating by that not a dis-mattered, ethereal body, but a body that is completely inspired and animated by God's Spirit (*pneuma*) of life and love (1 Cor. 15:44). In another letter Paul says that a life powered by the Spirit results in "love, joy, peace, patience, kindness, generosity, faithfulness, gentleness, and self-control" (Gal. 5:22–23). These "fruits of the Spirit" stand as a critique of our normal ways of living and as a promise of the good that is yet to be. Difficult as it is for us to imagine, a resurrected body moves only as love and never as fear or hate or boredom.

The crucial thing to note is that a resurrected body is still a material body, however transformed, in continuity with the bodies we
are now. The moment it ceases to be material is the moment when
love's way of life has been replaced by some creation-denying, dual-
istic form of evasion or escape.

The gospel of Luke reports that Jesus appeared to his disciples
in his resurrected body, blessed them, withdrew, and "was carried
up into heaven." The disciples worshipped him and "returned to
Jerusalem with great joy; and they were continually in the temple
blessing God" (24:50–53). In the gospel of John Jesus appears to his
disciples in his resurrected body and then sends them out into the
world with a message of peace and a mission of feeding. He does not
send them out under their own steam, however. In a scene remarkably reminiscent of the creation narrative in Genesis, where God's
spirit hovers over everything to bring it to life, Jesus breathes on
them the Holy Spirit, a spirit that enables them to forgive and thus
liberate others into new forms of life (20:22–23). And in the book
of Acts the resurrected Jesus appeared to his disciples, gave them
instructions, and then "was lifted up, and a cloud took him out of
their sight" (1:9).

These accounts are fascinating because they communicate, first,
that resurrection life pertains to and is committed to the life of this
world, so that it can be put on a better path, and, second, that Jesus
did not remain in this world but was carried up into heaven. The
first point is confirmed by the fact that the disciples are not to hide
away or withdraw, but do the work of spreading Jesus's loving way
of life in the world and build his body, the church, so that all can
enjoy the membership of mutual nurture and support. They will do
this under the inspiration and the power of the Holy Spirit, a spirit
that guides people in the ways of love.

The second point, described by tradition as Christ's "ascension"
to heaven, has sometimes been a source of embarrassment for Christians, because it suggests a mythological, prescientific way of think-

ing in which heaven exists "up somewhere beyond the blue." Is Jesus's ascension a form of escape, and thus a refutation of all that I have been saying about heaven as the healing rather than evasion of this world?

The first thing to note is that Jesus does not ascend with his soul alone. His ascension to heaven is a bodily ascension. If ascension entailed Jesus's leaving his body behind, that would amount to another form of dualism that posits the immortality of the soul (the same point can be made about the resurrection: if Christians subscribed to dualism, Jesus's body should have been in the tomb on Easter Sunday; if Jesus's body was in the tomb, then Christians have lost their hope).

Ascension does not undermine the goodness of material creation. Instead, it represents the fulfillment of it, because as Jesus ascends in his body, he communicates that *embodiment and materiality are taken into the life of heaven.* Heaven is not closed to material bodies or to earth or flesh! It can't be, because every created thing is the expression of God's love. God's desire is to be with the creatures. It is not to see them destroyed. That means *heaven is not closed to bodies but only to sin,* which is the power that distorts and degrades bodies. Not all bodies ascend with Jesus at this time, because they can't yet: they are still under the sway of confused loves and thus susceptible to the wounding of this world. Only those bodies that are resurrected, that is, only those bodies fully animated by God's spirit, can experience the life of heaven, because heaven is the place where love alone is the power that moves life.

That Jesus is described as going "up" and away from earth should not be understood in literal fashion, as if heaven really is some location beyond earth's stratosphere. It is helpful here to think of differing dimensions of reality, differing kinds of worlds. Heaven is not "of this world" not because it is immaterial, but because the kinds of relationships operative in our time and place are still too much governed by violation and wounding. Our reality as it is now is not yet compatible with the reality of peace and joy that God has in store for it. Jesus, therefore, has to leave this material world not because he disdains materiality, but because the social world as it is now does not yet fully embrace or manifest his resurrection life and love. Jesus's ascension confirms that the world as we organize it is still too much under the direction of sin. His ascension is confirmation that another world is possible and awaits us, because God's love is constantly at work.

What his followers are told is that Jesus will return (Acts 1:11) and that with his return he will bring the nurturing, celebratory life of heaven fully into the life of this material world. At this moment the whole of reality, material and social, will be healed, so that every creature can fully experience and enjoy love's way of life. At this moment the whole of creation will become new, because God's love will be "all in all." That's a vision worth participating in and working toward. That is the vision that funds Christian hope.

CHAPTER 14

The Harmonies of Heaven

You have made known to me the ways of life; you will make me
full of gladness with your presence.
ACTS 2:28, REFERENCING PSALM 16:8–11

A s CHRISTIANS TRIED TO describe what heavenly life meant and
practically entailed, they turned to Jesus Christ. Jesus is the one who
saves people from a life that ends in loneliness and alienation, pain
and violence. He does this by inviting people to share in his life and
in so doing experience all that God makes possible in creation. Jesus
offers life in all its abundance, but in order for people to experience
this life they must live "in him." In other words, they must learn to
share in his ministries of companionship, feeding, healing, exorcising, and reconciling, because these ministries create the conditions
in which creatures can savor a taste of the life of heaven. When
we remember that heaven is about the full healing of rather than

an escape from this world, then we can turn our attention to the repair and reconciliation of relationships that make every life possible. Heaven is the place of reconciled relationships. That means it is also the place where harmony rules.

The apostle Paul described the dawning of heavenly life when he said, "So if anyone is in Christ, there is a new creation: everything old has passed away; see, everything has become new!" (2 Cor. 5:17). When Paul makes reference to a "new creation," he is talking about the *reconciliation* of the whole cosmos (in Rom. 8:18–23 he speaks of Christ's saving action as *liberating* creatures from the degrading contexts they find themselves in). Creation as it is now needs liberating and reconciling, because it has become a place of degradation and destruction. Too many creatures find themselves in oppressive contexts, compelled to live in ways that frustrate and thwart their potential. But this is not their ultimate destiny. God wants all creation to be reconciled and whole. "All this is from God, who reconciled us to himself through Christ, and has given us the ministry of reconciliation; that is, in Christ God was reconciling the world (*cosmos*) to himself, not counting their trespasses against them, and entrusting the message of reconciliation to us" (5:18–19).

Whatever the details of heavenly life are, it is clear that creatures living in reconciled relationship with each other and with God will be at its core. Heaven is about ending the estrangement, hostility, and envy and the fear, boredom, and shame that keep us separated from and at odds with each other.

In one of the church's earliest proclamations of faith Christians said an astounding thing about Jesus and the wide, all-inclusive scope of his work:

He [Jesus] is the image of the invisible God, the firstborn
of all creation; for in him all things in heaven and on earth
were created, things visible and invisible, whether thrones or
dominions or rulers or powers—all things have been created

through him and for him. He himself is before all things, and
in him all things hold together. He is the head of the body, the
church; he is the beginning, the firstborn from the dead, so that
he might come to have first place in everything. For in him the
fullness of God was pleased to dwell, and through him God
was pleased to reconcile to himself all things, whether on earth
or in heaven, by making peace through the blood of his cross.
(Col. 1:15–20)

The love of Jesus circulates *through everything* as the power to heal
and bring wholeness of life, because it is only this love that enables
creation to finally hold together and flourish. Nothing escapes Jesus's reconciling work, because every creature plays an indispensable
role in the life of all the others. That means, then, that as the church
takes on his reconciling work as its own, it too must attend to the
healing of the whole world. The message of reconciliation and the
reality of heaven are never confined to humans. They extend to "all
things, whether on earth or in heaven," which is why it is necessary
for the gospel "good news" to be proclaimed "to every creature
under heaven" (Col. 1:23).

This is a vision of heaven that has peace at its core. Jesus makes
peace possible, because he unleashes the sort of love that inspires
people to offer themselves to each other. Following his own self-
sacrificing path, Christians learn that peace is not reducible to the
"end of hostilities" or some kind of benign neglect. It is, rather,
an active disposition that has the flourishing of communities as its
focus. Jesus reconciles by being the kind of presence that strengthens
relationships by putting people into a position where they can better
love one another.

Another way to think about love's reconciling presence is to
characterize it as a *harmonizing* presence. In a heavenly world dis-
sonant relationships have been transformed into harmonious ones.
Paul alludes to this in his letter to the Christians at Ephesus when

he says that those filled with the Spirit of Christ's love will sing together in ways that are melodious and give thanks to God (Eph. 5:18–20). Why does harmonious and grateful singing together serve as a sign that life is being lived "in Christ"? To answer this question we need to turn to the dynamics of musical performance.

Training in Harmony

FOR HARMONIOUS SOUND TO emerge, a spirit of hospitality must penetrate and animate those gathered to sing; there must be a spirit of welcome that makes room for another's sound and a spirit of nurture that helps them to sing at their best. In a harmonious world, no one is discarded and no one's sound is discordant. Instead, all are brought together such that their being together creates a full and beautiful sound.

What I mean is beautifully expressed in Kay Pollak's 2004 film *As It Is in Heaven*. Set in a small Swedish village, this film is the story of some residents who form a choir. The conductor is Daniel Daréus, a once world-famous musician and conductor, recently returned to his childhood home to recover from exhaustion and emotional collapse.

At the first practice he quickly sees that the road ahead will be difficult: there is a lot of dissension, rivalry, and distrust in the group. They don't know how to be together in ways that nurture and inspire each other to be better than they could be if they remain alone. Daniel tells the choir members that everything begins with listening. He says, "Imagine that all music already exists. It's up here, all around, vibrating, ready to be taken down. It's all a matter of listening, of being ready to take it down. Each person has their own unique tone, their own individual tone. And we're going to find it."

Needless to say, choir members are puzzled about what he could possibly mean. They are easily distracted by their cell phones and the worries of their lives. So at the next practice Daniel starts with their bodies, encouraging them to stretch and massage their bellies, so they can be loosened up to receive and respond to the vibrations going on around them. He then has them lie down on the floor in an arrangement of heads resting on bellies, so that they can feel each other's breathing. Finding this exercise ridiculous, they can't stop laughing.

Daniel wants them to know that they can't sing together if they are not first listening to each other, feeling the vibrations of each other through the intimacy of touching bodies and shared breathing. To produce the harmony that complements each other, they must first be deeply *attuned* to each other. He gathers them in a circle to hold hands and hum. He wants them to hear each other's voices and find where they are in relation to each other. For a symphony of sound to emerge, they must first learn to be deeply sympathetic to each other.

Though these people had lived with each other for many years, it is clear that they do not know each other deeply. Their lives are not lived in resonant sympathy with each other. Gabriella is regularly beaten by her husband Connie, but choir members have not entered into her fear and pain with her. Lena seems to be switching boyfriends every week, but no one understands or sympathizes with her pain of being betrayed by a married man she had come to love. Inger is deeply unhappy in her marriage, but she, let alone others, hardly knows it. Arne is blinded by the arrogance of his own ambition and unaware that he is hurting others to elevate himself. He regularly makes fun of Holmfrid, calling him "Fatso," not realizing that this taunt has made Holmfrid's life one of self-loathing and insecurity. Arne doesn't want Tore, a mentally handicapped young man, to join the group, because it will ruin the dream he has about their becoming a great choir.

One day during rehearsal as they are trying to sing "Amazing Grace," it is clear to Daniel that they can't harmonize. He stops the singing and asks what is wrong. He wants them to consider what is wrong interpersonally, because he understands that symphonic, harmonious sound depends on singers who live in sympathetic, supportive relationship with each other. Siv announces that she is displeased with Lena and that she disapproves of her lifestyle. She can't be in tune with a person she believes to be living an immoral life. Arne laughs at the admission. Siv eventually leaves the choir because of her anger and jealousy.

Time spent together rehearsing and attending to each other is gradually having a good effect. Choir members are learning to be with each other in supportive and playful ways. They are seeing what it means to love each other, even if they don't always follow through. Slowly a beautiful sound is emerging from their singing, a harmonious sound made possible by the affections of love. And so plans are made to present a spring concert for the community.

Daniel has composed a special song for Gabriella to sing, but she is terrified to offer her voice in this way. She has been beaten down so much by Connie that she no longer believes she has a voice worth hearing. She has not yet known the love of others prepared to support her as she ventures forth. Encouraged by choir members, however, she takes the risk. At the concert she sings beautifully about how she wants to feel alive all her living days: "I want to feel I'm alive knowing I was good enough." When they are finished, the community erupts in cheers. Choir members are beaming, because together they sound good. They are also so happy to have helped Gabriella find her voice and the sense that her life matters and is valued.

It was risky for Gabriella to offer her voice, not only because of the potential embarrassment of singing out of tune. What if others laughed at what she presented? What if their rejection of her performance was really a rejection of her? It is not to be taken for granted that Gabriella would be able to sing beautifully, especially when we see how she lived in fear. Why should she take the brave step and offer her voice to her community in song when her abusive husband had beaten her down so often?

Gabriella could sing triumphantly, because she felt the nurturing embrace of her fellow choir members. She trusted that they would not let her fall or leave her stranded. They, in turn, trusted her to give her best. They saw in her potential that she did not see in herself. In a harmonious choir people are dependent on each other in a most intimate way; they develop their voices by joining them to the voices of others, breath mingling with breath. That makes harmony a fragile and vulnerable thing. There is no guarantee that beautiful sound will emerge from this sympathetic and symbiotic effort. It only takes one person to lose faith, only one to break fidelity with the group, for the effort to slowly come apart.

The Communal Conditions for Harmony

HARMONIOUS SINGING IS NOT about the promotion of one's own agenda. It is about listening and witnessing to the life we share together. Blues, jazz, country, rock, bluegrass, hip-hop, rap, orchestral, baroque, classical, and more—all are essential forms of music; the variety is needed to express the depth and breadth, the pain and the anger, and the joy and ecstasy of our life together. Singing is an improvisational gesture that replies to and comes alongside others. For this to go well, attention and restraint are crucial, as is submission to the truth of what is happening and trying to be expressed. The submission is important because it affirms the communal context of sound—the shared air and in-spiration that we all breathe, the sigh and the shout—what we might also call the rhythmic harmonies of music. When this communal context is respected and nurtured, only then can each individual voice be heard in all its integrity, beauty, and profundity. If every voice present tried to dominate, the result would be noise, and thus would each note be diminished. Attending to the communal context of sound enables us to appreciate what can be called the hospitable character of music.

It is tempting to shy away from harmonious life for fear that in joining with another the integrity of each will be compromised. Thinking that coming together is a zero-sum game, the worry, perhaps, is that the one will be diminished at the expense of the other or even disappear in the mingling of the two (think here of how red and yellow disappear when mixed, yielding orange). But if we think musically rather than visually, an entirely different possibility emerges.

In the sounding of two notes at the same time, the one does not drive the other away, nor does it simply merge with another to make something else. Instead, each sound is distinct and able to be heard. Coming together, they can do what they could not do alone, namely, make the sound of a chord that exists in addition to the sounds of the individual notes. This chord creates a new sound, which also gives to each single note fresh possibilities for expression and hearing. What happens is that the discrete tones *sound through each other* and interpenetrate each other. As my friend and colleague Jeremy Begbie puts it, "They can be *in* one another, while being heard *as* two distinct tones."[1] With the sounding of a chord the integrity of each sound is not only preserved, but enhanced.

The key to all of this is that the notes *resonate* with each other. In a situation of resonance the sounding of one note (middle C) will automatically call forth the sympathetic sounding of its corresponding harmonic note (upper C). The tones are not in competition. They establish each other, free each other to be what they are, and actually enhance the rich potential latent within each note. What their coming together does is create a larger, more inclusive sound, a sound that can expand outward as it attracts a sympathetic response from others. Theologian David Ford calls this the "performance of abundance":

> Sounds do not have exclusive boundaries—they can blend,
> harmonize, resonate with each other in endless ways. In
> singing there can be a filling of space with sound in ways that
> draw more and more voices to take part, yet with no sense of
> crowding. It is a performance of abundance, as new voices join
> in with their distinctive tones. . . . The music is both inside
> and outside them, and it creates a new vocal, social space of
> community in song.[2]

Musical harmony shows us how two or more entities coming together—whether individual notes or individual people—can produce something more, while at the same time enhancing the individual. The goal is not to diminish or stifle an individual's life. It is, rather, to position selves with each other, so that their being together unleashes the full potential of each individual, while at the same time enriching the life of the whole. That is what the experience of heaven will do. It is an experience that is so much more than simply getting along. In heaven the lives of individuals are not threatened, but rather strengthened and enhanced by the presence of others. In heaven each life attains the fullness of what it can be.

I saw this up close when I sang under my mother-in-law, Harriet Ziegenhals, the founder and director of Chicago's Community Renewal Chorus and All God's Children, both interracial and multi-ethnic choirs. She understood as well as any conductor I have known that the heart of a good chorus is a community of singers who care for each other and seek to be harmonious in their shared lives as much as in their shared singing, which is why she spent so much of her time ministering to her singers and helping them minister to each other. In one of her weekly handwritten letters to the choir she observed:

We are members for a greater purpose. We work and sing together so that in some way (1) we can make our city a better place in which to live; (2) we can bring some measure of understanding to those who hear us of the meaning of community in a time when community is being destroyed by polarization; and (3) through community we hope to encourage reconciliation, justice, and peace.

To become a harmonious community, however, takes commitment over the long haul:

When you have shared with one another more than a decade of joys, illnesses, births, deaths, weddings, and funerals, you are bound together in a deeper way than just the bond of singing together each Tuesday and Saturday. When gathered prayer has helped to bring about miracles, you become involved in another's life.

And so when Jody sang "Lady Bug" Saturday night, we cheered and applauded not only because it was so beautifully sung, but because we remember the first time she sang it as a little girl and again as a teenager at Orchestra Hall, and we remember her struggling through good and bad times in her life in between.

And when "Dr. John" sang "Wher'er You Walk," we cheered not only because of the beauty of his voice and interpretation, but because we are proud to have this fine physician as one of us and remember his kindness and patience as "our doc" all through Europe.

And we applaud Jose Huerta and Dave Bergstrom, because they were *good* and because they are our smallest and tallest new members, and we wanted them to feel welcome too.

A choir animated by the Spirit of Christ's love retains the

memory of each member within it, because each member has played an indispensable role in the formation, functioning, and flourishing of the group. To forget even one is to misrepresent what the choir has been and what it might yet potentially be:

> **Every single CRC/AGC choir member is valued and needed. Every person is important. No one is just a number or a file folder, but a contributing human being. You are each a unique individual. No one else can bring to the choir your special skills and talents, your sense of humor, your special heritage and background. . . . We find strength in our diversity—we seldom if ever get bored with one another! Through the power of music we receive back 100-fold all we contribute.**[3]

It is no accident that Harriet ends her letter with an expression of gratitude to each and every member for having shared their lives with the choir and with the world. Shared life is the best life, because it acknowledges how we need each other and how we can be a help to each other. To sing together is to hear and feel how we need each other's breath, that most intimate, animating region of our being. And it is to experience the elevation of each other, as voices crescendo in harmonious fulfillment.

These insights from music help us understand what it means to be the "body of Jesus Christ," that unique, social, singing body called by God to witness to God's continuing saving and redeeming presence on earth. Paul affirms that this body consists of many diverse members (or notes), each of which has a special talent to contribute to the flourishing and harmonizing of the group. When the Spirit of love is at work in them, what they do will be "for the common good" (1 Cor. 12:7). In other words, the breath that circulates through them will be the self-offering Spirit of Christ (in Hebrew "spirit" and "breath" come from the same word, *ruah*). As baptized members they will be joined to each other not with the aim of first seeking their own benefit, but rather seeking the well-being of the membership, because it is the membership that creates the communal space in which members can be nurtured to more fully become themselves. There must be no arrogance or dissension in Christ's body. Instead, each person should seek the well-being of others. So closely interdependent are they, so closely have they joined their feeling and desires to each other, that "if one member suffers, all suffer together with it; if one member is honored, all rejoice together with it" (1 Cor. 12:26). It is hard not to see Gabriella in this verse.

Love is the power that enables people to make the movements of a singing community. It is the discipline and the disposition that equips people to give themselves to others, so that they can fully realize the potential God has given them. It creates the communal contexts of nurture that are crucial to people who are prepared to risk the journeys of self- and world discovery. Love is the hospitable and merciful way of being that makes room within us to welcome others as gifts rather than threats. It inspires us to be patient with each other, recognizing that each person comes to life wounded and worried, hurt and hesitant. But in gently waiting upon each other and in accepting responsibility for each other, the possibility of a beautiful and fulfilled life emerges. Paul put it directly:

> Love is patient; love is kind; love is not envious or boastful or arrogant or rude. It does not insist on its own way; it is not irritable or resentful; it does not rejoice in wrongdoing, but rejoices in the truth. It bears all things, believes all things, hopes all things, endures all things. Love never ends. (1 Cor. 13:4–8)

Once again, imagine for a moment what your life would be like if the people you knew were each devoted to helping you find and then exercise your gifts, thereby helping you realize all that is best in your life. Then imagine yourself becoming sympathetic to the lives of others and committing to be an encouraging, nurturing presence. What is being imagined is something of the life of heaven, a life in which God is glorified in the abundant, flowering life of each thing.

What Makes It Heaven

ENOUGH HAS BEEN SAID to determine that heaven is not some specific location far, far away. If it were, then the primary issue would be one of figuring out how to get from here (earth) to there (heaven). People would then have to identify the correct map or set of teachings or seek out the institutional gatekeepers who can provide them with the ticket that will secure their passage. The key would be to find out what needs to be done now—go to church, put money in an offering plate, do nice things, have faith, or some variation on these—to attain the ticket. Upon arrival, all the pain people have known and felt will simply disappear.

The problem with this scenario is that it completely overlooks the more fundamental matter: it is not *where we are* but *how we are wherever we are* that determines one's entrance into heaven. It does people no good whatsoever to make a trip to some heavenly place, if they have not first been transformed into people who cherish and celebrate the gift of where they are. Failing this transformation, people will simply enter into the next paradise and do what they did to the first paradise in Eden: they will degrade and destroy it on their way to self-protection and self-promotion. What makes a place genuinely a place that people love and feel they belong to is not so much the *location* but the *quality of relationships* that are going on there. If this is true, then we need to think less about *where* heaven is and more about *how* we are living wherever we are. Heaven is any place where the relationships between all those who are there are permeated by the love of Jesus. Heaven is the place where there is no shame and people can sing beautifully and harmoniously.

Similarly, "eternal life" is not simply unending life or the interminable extension of life as we now know it (which for some people might be a living hell!). Rather, it is the time when people become fully present to the moment, because they have given themselves in love to the love of God that is present there. Eternal life is the fullness of time, the time when people completely connect to the love of God before them and so want to give themselves unreservedly to it in a return gesture of love. There is no past or future in this time, because where one is and who one is with are completely satisfying. Eternity is when people live harmoniously into the wholeness of life, realizing that everything and everyone are gifts to be cherished and enjoyed. Past and future disappear, because there is no other place or time one could possibly want to be.

This means that heaven, rather than being about one's entrance into a specific location, is about one's entrance into a transformed life. More specifically, *it is about one's full participation in love's way of life.* To see what I mean, we can turn to Revelation, the last book in scripture. Admittedly, Revelation, owing to its dense and highly symbolic content, has given rise to all sorts of notorious speculation about the predicted end of the world, much of it peppered with agony and conflagration, much of it silly because of the desire to map an ideological agenda onto today's political or geographical realities. But Revelation is not about the destruction of the space-time universe. It is, rather, about the coming to an end of the violent orders of this world (especially as seen in the oppressive power of Rome) that wound and destroy, so that God's way of love and peace might come to rule. As has already been said, "the end" is not about humanity's escape from earth, but God's permanent descent to be with creatures and lead them in the ways of joy and peace.

In order for God to make a home among mortals and then dwell with them (Rev. 21:3), it is essential that the material world be transformed, so that in all of its characteristics life can flourish and flower. This is what love demands. It would be a contradiction for perfected love to live side by side with degradation, disease, and death. And so, not surprisingly, Revelation describes a new earth in which ecological and biological processes have been purified and healed: "Then the angel showed me the river of the water of life, bright as crystal, flowing from the throne of God and of the Lamb through the middle of the street of the city. On either side of the river is the tree of life with its twelve kinds of fruit, producing its fruit each month; and the leaves of the tree are for the healing of the nations. Nothing accursed will be found there anymore" (22:1–3).

What Revelation describes is a world that has been wounded but is now healed, because it is in direct communication with the life-giving power of God. All people from every corner of the world have gathered together and share in the nurturing, refreshing fruit that God provides. Life now becomes for them an "eternal banquet" and an "unending Sabbath" in which the gifts of God are freely shared and fully enjoyed.

The writer of Revelation paints a vision in which God, by coming to dwell with creatures, makes all things new (21:5). The old ways of relating have come to an end because they are ways that result in pain, tears, and death. How does this happen? It happens because people are living a life that is "in Christ," a life in which their seeing, hearing, touching, smelling, and tasting—their overall mode of feeling for others—is thoroughly inspired and shaped by the love of God. Revelation says that in this holy place there will no longer be a sun or moon, because God will be the light by which everything is seen (21:23; 22:5). No longer is anything perceived or engaged from an anxious or self-serving point of view. Instead, everything is welcomed and received as God does: as precious, as beautiful, and as worthy of love and celebration. Love's way of life is now installed and made permanent as the only way to be.

This is an arresting vision. Is it a fairy tale? Everything depends on whether you trust Jesus to have shown humanity what love really looks like and requires. It depends on whether you find the drama of love as Christianity understands it compelling. What it really comes down to is whether you believe that love is not a ruse.

This picture of the world's end does not stand alone, but is the logical conclusion to the drama of love as I have tried to present it. Jesus shows us that love's *creation* of life leads, eventually and necessarily, to every creature's *healing* and *resurrection* into the heavenly life of God. God never abandons anything that God creates. Looking to Jesus, we see that all life is meaningful and precious and therefore worthy of our attention and care.

Creation is not the fluke effect of a random, meaningless process. Life is a miracle. It did not need to be. That it is is the daily reminder that everything depends on the hospitable, nurturing, liberating, and empowering love of God. Which is to say, finally, that love is a miracle too.

Epilogue: Moving On in Love

CHRISTIANS HAVE IT ON good authority that *faith without works is dead*. What they sometimes forget is that *faith without love is deadly*, because the works performed without love frequently bring about needless suffering and pain.

This point needs repeating again and again, since it is so easy for people of faith to lose their focus and way. When Christians forget that the drama of life is founded upon and centered around love, they soon find themselves committing to programs and plans that hurt rather than heal, divide rather than reconcile, deprive rather than nurture. It would be a good idea to constantly reconsider the famous words from the apostle Paul:

> Love is patient; love is kind; love is not envious or boastful or arrogant or rude. It does not insist on its own way; it is not irritable or resentful; it does not rejoice in wrongdoing, but rejoices in the truth. It bears all things, believes all things, hopes all things, endures all things. Love never ends. (1 Cor. 13:4–8)

These are not comforting words. They are, in reality, terrifying, because they serve as the daily reminder of how easy it is to fail to love. They call our attention to the fact that we so readily replace

233

love with impatience, meanness, bullying, envy, arrogance, resentment . . . the list goes on and on.

Scripture poses the question: "Can faith save you?" (James 2:14). It is an important question, particularly in a time of John 3:16 Christianity, when many claim that all people have to do is "believe on Jesus" and they will have eternal life. The writer of James wants to bring this train of thought to a stop, because he thinks it results in hypocritical people and worthless religion. Christianity that is true and worthy of the name results in people who care for each other and for those in distress. Faith that is genuine leads to the love of one's neighbors and the care of their bodily needs.

Faith and work, faith and love—these are not in opposition to each other. But the primacy goes to love, because it is love that provides the *why* and *what for* of faith and work. One could even say that the principal aim of faith, its reason for being, is to prepare the time and space in which love can fully go to work. Love is the inspiration, means, and goal of all life. Faith and work, trust and discipline, piety and learning— these matter only insofar as they facilitate and express this love. And love needs all of them to come to full fruition, because love is hard.

Consider the gospel parable of the father and his two sons (Luke 15:11–32). The younger son decides he wants his inheritance early. He leaves home and quickly squanders it all on excessive living. Finding himself without money and food, he is reduced to feeding pigs in a field. He is so hungry and so desperate that he longs to eat what the pigs are eating, but no one is giving him anything. He decides to return to his father, hoping to receive at least what his hired laborers get.

His father is a compassionate man and has been waiting, perhaps even longing, for the wayward son to return. Upon his return, the father showers him with kisses, outfits him with fine clothes, and throws a feast in celebration. The older son, however, is not so happy. Though he has worked hard for his father many years, his brother, the one who was prodigal with the family's wealth, is being celebrated in a way that he, the faithful one, never has. The father's love brings relief and joy to the younger son, but it causes anger and resentment in the older. The parable ends with the father pleading with his older son to join the celebration and rejoice in the life of his lost brother. We are left to wonder whether the father rejoins the party and whether the older son joins in at all.

There is enough ambiguity in this story, enough unsaid, for us to appreciate the difficulty of love. How could the younger son be so ungrateful, so cavalier, and so presumptuous with his father's wealth and then think that his father would take him back? Will he finally learn to give of himself or will he always be the one who takes? How will the older son deal with his resentment at being slighted and forgotten by his father? Will he get over the sense that he is morally justified in his contempt of his younger brother? And how will the father deal with the knowledge that his compassion for his younger son has brought such pain to his older son? What will it take for them to be a family, a convivial home, and a membership of mutual nurture, respect, and celebration?

We are left with the image of the father pleading with his older son. It is a good image to keep in mind, because it is the posture of pleading and the determination to stick with each other—especially in the midst of confusion and pain—that we most need as we try to make progress in the ways of love. Moving forward we are going to need the sorts of engagement in which people are committed to being truthful and merciful with each other, so that we can see where love has failed and where love yet needs to grow.

In the course of daily life it is fairly easy for people to get into routines that keep them more or less closed within themselves. People are out and about, but the occasions are fairly rare in which they are confronted with people or situations that challenge their assumptions about love. It is tempting to hang out mostly with people who are like us, have similar backgrounds, read the same things, and expect similar things out of life. With today's on-demand culture and the many diverse media outlets now available, we can go through life hardly ever having to deal with those who are genuinely other, are in need, or strongly disagree with us. In contexts like these, love runs the risk of becoming naive and sentimental.

Which is why we need to seek out opportunities for deep and sustained engagement with the diverse places of this world and its many peoples and then accept personal responsibility for the well-being of each neighborhood and region. The task ahead is to commit to building beloved communities in which the flourishing of all creatures is the central focus. It is to join the diverse memberships of life, really dig in, and commit to being a merciful, nurturing, and forgiving presence.

Sometimes the places of our engagement will have been ravaged by war and ethnic hatred and so need the courage and witness of someone like Maggy or the ministry Freely in Hope to bring healing and reconciliation. Sometimes it will be a plot of land, like The Lord's Acre, that needs the skill and compassion of someone like Susan to restore nurture and beauty. Or it might be a local congregation like Faith Baptist Church, which rallied around Mark and his family and so witnessed to the commitment to be a daily source of help and encouragement even when the medical prognosis is grim.

The task is not to be a hero or to develop the coolest new program that will unleash love as it's never been seen before. The work ahead will be much humbler than that, because it will begin in confession and with the prayer that we become honest about our failure to love. It will move gently and mercifully and with the hope each of us will become more attentive to and patient with others and with the places in which we live. It will have as its end a wide assortment of communities in which diverse people eat, sing, and dance with each other.

What love desires is intimacy and the flourishing of those it touches—this is what life as the drama of love teaches. In and through and for love, God creates a hospitable world and then invites each person to join in the welcome, nurture, and celebration of everyone and everything. Life as love. I cannot imagine a more important vocation or a more worthy goal.

ACKNOWLEDGMENTS

T HE IDEA FOR THIS book came out of teaching a yearlong course at Duke Divinity School called "Inhabiting the Christian Drama." In it I wanted students to appreciate that Christianity is ultimately a drama centered on God's love for the world and all its creatures. My initial thanks, therefore, go to the first cohort of Master of Arts in Christian Studies students who engaged this course with such enthusiasm. Besides providing me with one of my most pleasing teaching experiences ever, they helped convince me that a presentation of Christianity as a drama of love made sense and was compelling. This book would not have happened without them.

A syllabus and lecture notes, however, do not make a book. In the writing of this book I have been helped by so many people who helped me think more clearly about its structure and content. First on this list is Mickey Maudlin at HarperOne. Mickey had faith in this project and gave me wise counsel throughout its writing. Thank you! His assistant Anna Paustenbach also read the manuscript in draft form and gave me valuable suggestions for improvement. Then there are the friends and colleagues who along the way read drafts of chapters or the whole thing: Fred Bahnson, Ellen Davis, Lisa Eddy, Stanley Hauerwas, Judith Heyhoe, Greg Jones, Rick Lischer, Susan Sides, David Toole, Hannah Ward, Lauren Winner, Anna Wirzba, Emily Wirzba, and Gretchen Ziegenhals. Special thanks, too, to Diana Butler Bass who agreed to write a Foreword to this book. Each gave generously of their time and insight, and I am so grateful. This book is better because of them.

Finally, I would like to thank The Louisville Institute, the Henry Luce Foundation, and the Association of Theological Schools for providing me with fellowships that enabled me to dedicate the time to reflect upon and write this book.

NOTES

CHAPTER 1: THE RIGHT MEASURE OF FAITH

1. As quoted in Kevin Clarke, *Oscar Romero: Love Must Win Out* (Collegeville, MN: Liturgical, 2014), 16.

CHAPTER 2: LOVE LESSONS

1. Quoted in the memorial to Brother Luc available at http://www.findagrave .com/cgi-bin/fg.cgi?page=gr&GRid=62787858. This brief memorial provides a sketch of Brother Luc's life.
2. My telling of the story of Brother Luc and the monks at Tibhirine is indebted to John W. Kiser's *The Monks of Tibhirine: Faith, Love, and Terror in Algeria* (New York: St. Martin's Press, 2002). This quote and the following from Brother Christian appear on p. 245. The story of these monks has been made into the 2011 motion picture *Of Gods and Men,* directed by Xavier Beauvois.
3. Kiser, *The Monks of Tibhirine,* 199.

CHAPTER 4: WHEN LOVE BECOMES FLESH, LIFE IS CREATED

1. Julian of Norwich, *Showings* (Mahwah, NJ: Paulist Press, 1978), Long Text, chap. 5, 183.

Chapter 5: Creation Garden Style

1.   Emma's story comes from personal communication with Susan Sides. I am grateful to Susan for allowing me to share it. Fred Bahnson has also written insightfully about The Lord's Acre and its significance in *Soil and Sacrament: A Spiritual Memoir of Food and Faith* (New York: Simon & Schuster, 2013).

Chapter 6: The Feast of Creation: On Learning Hospitality

1.   Robert Farrar Capon, *The Supper of the Lamb: A Culinary Reflection* (New York: Modern Library, 1967), 189.
2.   Isak Dinesen, "Babette's Feast," in *Anecdotes of Destiny and Ehrengard* (New York: Vintage, 1993). This story is also available online at http://www.sfa-auvillar.com/GOUT/2012_03_vienne_autriche/documents/le-diner-de-babette_ENGLISH.pdf. My references are from the online edition.
3.   Capon, *Supper of the Lamb,* 40.
4.   Capon, *Supper of the Lamb,* 85–86.
5.   Capon, *Supper of the Lamb,* 114–15.
6.   Capon, *Supper of the Lamb,* 189.

Chapter 7: When Love Fails, Life Falls Apart

1.   Tracy Letts, *August: Osage County* (New York: Theater Communications Group, 2008), 123.
2.   Letts, *August: Osage County,* 96.
3.   Letts, *August: Osage County,* 48, 122.
4.   Letts, *August: Osage County,* 121.
5.   Letts, *August: Osage County,* 135.

Chapter 8: From Intimacy to Idolatry: The Origins of Sin

1.   Annie Dillard, *Pilgrim at Tinker Creek* (New York: Harper & Row, 1974).

Chapter 9: The Wide Reach of Sin

1.   My account of the Martin County disaster is based on Erik Reece's *Lost Mountain: A Year in the Vanishing Wilderness: Radical Strip Mining and the Devastation of Appalachia* (New York: Riverhead, 2006), 131.
2.   Reece, *Lost Mountain,* 126.
3.   Reece, *Lost Mountain,* 129.
4.   Harry M. Caudill, *Night Comes to the Cumberlands: A Biography of a Depressed Area* (Boston: Little, Brown, 1962), x.

5.   Bob Sloan, "For Love of Kentucky, Stop Destroying Her," in Kristin Jo-hannsen, Bobbie Ann Mason, and Mary Ann Taylor-Hall, eds., *Missing Mountains: We Went to the Mountaintop but It Wasn't There* (Nicholasville, KY: Wind Publications, 2005), 166, 168.

CHAPTER 10: WHEN LOVE GOES TO WORK, LIFE IS HEALED

1.   Mark Eddy's words are based on oral testimony given at Faith Baptist Church, Georgetown, Kentucky, on September 24, 2006. I am deeply grateful to Lisa Eddy for giving me permission to tell her family's story.

CHAPTER 11: THE COMMUNAL CONTEXTS OF HEALTH

1.   My telling of Eunice's story is from the Freely in Hope website, http://www.freelyinhope.org/portfolio/eunice/. Marion's response is described in an interview given at Leadership Education at Duke University Divinity School and is available at http://www.faithandleadership.com/qa/marion-ndeta-wasia-new-life-for-sexual-assault-victims-kenya?utm_source=newsletter&utm_medium=headline&utm_campaign=FL_feature.

2.   Nikole's story can be found at http://www.freelyinhope.org/about/founders-story/.

CHAPTER 12: LOVE CREATES A NEW WORLD

1.   "A Discussion with Marguerite Barankitse, Maison Shalom, Burundi," a 2011 interview conducted at Georgetown University's Berkley Center for Religion, Peace & World Affairs (http://berkleycenter.georgetown.edu/interviews/a-discussion-with-marguerite-barankitse-maison-shalom-burundi). I am greatly indebted to Judith Debetencourt Hoskins for information about Maggy and the many children she has helped. Her book *Hummingbird, Why Am I Here? Maggy's Children* (self-published, 2012) is an account of Maggy and her work at Maison Shalom. It is based on extensive interviews and provides much helpful information that I refer to throughout in my telling of Maggy's story.

2.   Quoted in Emmanuel Katongole's *The Sacrifice of Africa: A Political Theology for Africa* (Grand Rapids, MI: Eerdmans, 2011), 171. The quotation itself comes from Christel Martin's *La haine n'aura pas le derniere mot: Maggy la femme aux 10,000 enfants* [*Hate Won't Have the Last Word: Maggy the Woman with 10,000 Children*] (Paris: Albin Michel, 2005). My telling of Maggy's story has been greatly helped by Katongole and by Trent Dailey-Chwalibog and David Dimas's unpublished translation of Martin's book.

3.   Katongole, *Sacrifice of Africa*, 181–82.

4.   Katongole, *Sacrifice of Africa*, 182.

5.   "A Discussion with Marguerite Barankitse."

6.   Katongole, *Sacrifice of Africa*, 172.

7.   Katongole, *Sacrifice of Africa*, 190.

CHAPTER 13: WHEN LOVE IS ALL IN ALL, LIFE IS HEAVEN

1.   J. R. Baxter Jr., "This World Is Not My Home" (Dallas, TX: Stamps-Baxter Music and Printing, 1946).

2.   Wendell Berry, "Sabbaths VI, 2006," in *This Day: Sabbath Poems Collected and New 1979–2013* (Berkeley, CA: Counterpoint, 2013), 292–93.

CHAPTER 14: THE HARMONIES OF HEAVEN

1.   Jeremy Begbie, *Music, Modernity, and God: Essays in Listening* (Oxford: Oxford Univ. Press, 2013), 159.

2.   David F. Ford, *Self and Salvation: Being Transformed* (Cambridge: Cambridge Univ. Press, 1999), 121. In the writing of this section I have benefitted greatly from Ford's chapter "The Communication of God's Abundance: A Singing Self" and from conversation with Jeremy Begbie.

3.   Personal communication.

Scripture Index

SUBJECT INDEX

Aaron and the golden calf story, 121–22

actions: love of God as the power driving our, 37–39; of man creating disasters blamed on God, 136–38; Thomas Aquinas on God as the incomprehensible power or, 52; understanding that we will be accountable for our, 38

acts of God: examining acts of man directly leading to disasters called, 136–38; examining the logic of, 135–37; Logan County dam collapse (1972) blamed as, 134–35; Martin County coal sludge disaster (2000) blamed as, 131. *See also* God

Adam and Eve story: banishment from the Garden of Eden, 79, 127; on freedom to choose and restrain, 104, 114–17, 119–20; human sin reflected in the disobedience of, 40, 103–4; implications of our

refusal to receive the world as a gift in, 119–20; intimacy of love and rejection in, 110, 111–14

agency: Adam and Eve story on the ability to choose good and evil, 104, 114–17, 119–20; Jesus as demonstrating creation's reason and, 156–57; restraint as crucial to our exercise of freedom and, 155

Algeria: Brother Luc (Paul Dochier) and his lifetime service to people of, 25–29, 30–31; Paul Dochier's early service in, 25

All God's Children (Chicago chorus), 225–27

Apostles' Creed, 35

Appalachia mountains: John F. Kennedy's shock over the poverty and misery, 138; Martin County coal sludge disaster (2000) in, 131–34; mountaintop-removal (MTR) mining practice in the, 138–42;

compassion: healing by embracing
God's love and, 169; how fear and
insecurity erode, 98; Jesus as rep-
resentation of, 154, 172; prodigal
son parable on, 234–35
conditional love: damage of distorted
love of false expectations of, 105;
unconditional versus, 105–8
creation of the world: as the beginning of the drama of love, 50–51;
the Bible as beginning with a
seven–day creation poem on, 89;
characterized as a feast created by
God's love, 78–91; Christian faith
as beginning with God's, 40, 41;
as created from nothing but love,
51–55; as *ex amore* ("from love")
teaching of, 51; as *ex nihilo* ("from
nothing") teaching of, 51, 52, 54;
a garden as best example of, 61,
78; as God's hospitality service,
78–91; God's love as delighting in
the goodness of, 89, 90; Julian of
Norwich on God's, 47; the love of
God as explanation for the, 47–50,
74–75; perceiving God's gift of
the, 55–59; the Psalmist description of the, 71–73; as a teaching
about the character of the world
and life, 50; temptation to degrade
and deny God's, 56–57; understanding that love alone is the
foundation of, 48. *See also* gardens;
material world
crippled woman healed story, 153

Daréus, Daniel (*As It Is in Heaven*
character), 220–22
delight: *Babette's Feast* (Dinesen) as
story on sharing hospitality and,
82–88, 90–91; of Garden of Eden,
73, 80, 140; as goal of life, 90; of
God in the creation, 74, 75, 79,
80, 89; God's hospitality creating

conditions for, 113; how God's
love brings about, 48, 50, 53, 71;
of intimacy, 113; Noah's arch as
school for learning, 80; as part of
shalom, 70; the Sabbath meant to
share in God's, 89–90
demon-possessed man story, 153
Dillard, Annie, 117–18
Dinesen, Isak, 82, 86, 87
disembodied souls idea, 209–10
distorted love. *See* love's distortion
Dochier, Paul (Brother Luc), 25
dramas of love: completion in heaven
and hope, 40, 42; creation of
the world, 40, 41, 47–59, 61–75,
77–91; the fall and sin, 40, 41,
95–127, 129–42; the fourfold
structure and, 40–43; hope and
completion in heaven, 40, 42,
199–232; hope and completion in
heaven as ultimate purpose of the,
200–203; redemption and salvation, 40, 41–42, 145–57, 159–96.
See also love

eating: *Babette's Feast* (Dinesen) on
sharing delight of, 82–88, 90–91;
as daily demonstration of whether
we receive life as a gift, 124–25,
126–27; feeling of shame as-
sociated with, 126; as a healing
activity, 180–81; how today's food
industry denies the costly grace of
food and, 125–26; Peter's belief in
following the Jewish dietary codes
for, 181; as sometimes an occasion
for division, 180. *See also* hunger
Eddy, Lisa, 148
Eddy, Mark, 147–51, 236
Edward (rebel), 185
Emma and the missing melons story,
62–65, 71
environmental issues: challenge of
living harmoniously in the world,